LIVING *with* PAIN

LIVING *with* PAIN

Finding comfort in an uncomfortable world

JOEL PRICE

XULON PRESS

Xulon Press
2301 Lucien Way #415
Maitland, FL 32751
407.339.4217
www.xulonpress.com

Paperback ISBN-13: 978-1-66284-525-3
Ebook ISBN-13: 978-1-66284-533-8

TABLE OF CONTENTS

INTRODUCTION

I WAS RAISED to value toughness, and whether it was because of that upbringing or simply because of the way that I am wired, it stuck. I believe toughness, perseverance, and grit are critical characteristics needed to navigate this world well, but there is a trap when it comes to the development of these traits. Somewhere along the way you can confuse endurance and perseverance with denial. At least that is the trap I fell into.

I considered myself a tough person. Sure, I had experienced things that had caused me pain, but not like some people. I didn't have much to complain about, but I was strong enough to deal with what came my way. I would just lower my head and power through. I was tough. Or so I thought.

The problem is that denying the existence of the hurt you feel is not strength. It is cowardice. Strength is shown by facing pain and accepting that it exists in your life. Coping with pain takes strength. Denial is running away.

I didn't end up at that conclusion all at once. It was the result of many years and experiences, but I remember the moment it started to come together. Several years ago, I was sitting in church and thinking about pain. I had been wrestling with the idea of God as a comforter for the past several months, maybe even years. While I could rationalize my experience and point to others that seemingly had it worse than I did, I couldn't shake the fatigue. I felt like a beat dog, just waiting for the next blow to land. Life just kept coming at me.

Comforter? God? Frankly, I didn't buy it. I felt like someone at some point in history must have just missed a translation. God didn't seem like a comforter to me. When I thought of comfort, I thought of warm blankets and hot chocolate, or a puppy, or a really good hug. Comfort was a cozy thing. Comfort was soft and fuzzy. That just didn't sound like God. In no way could I conceive God as a puppy wrapped in a Snuggie, drinking cocoa, and offering me a hug.

I knew God. God was justice, mercy, and love. Justice wasn't warm. Mercy didn't evoke images of softness for me. Love? Maybe, but God's love seemed more like tough love, the kind of love that was good for me but didn't always feel good. And comfort was a feeling. Right? He wanted my best, but he loved me through discipline, trials, and forgiveness when I fell short. God's love seemed distant.

As I sat in church that day, I was wrestling with these thoughts. We had a guest preacher who suffered from chronic pain. Every day, all day, he was in pain, and he kept calling God the God of comfort. It made no sense. Here was a guy that literally dealt with pain on a daily basis. He made no bones about it. He was in pain. He didn't diminish it, but he also didn't show it. There was no moaning or calling attention to it. Yet, he acknowledged that it was bad and constant, and still, he called God the God of comfort. That sealed it for me. I was definitely missing something.

Now, I'm just a guy, probably a lot like you, a lot like all of us. I don't suffer from chronic pain. I'm not a survivor of a prisoner of war camp. I don't have a heroic story. So what gives me the right to author a book on pain?

Consider this: One in thirteen boys and one in four girls in America are sexually abused before they are eighteen[1]. There are over 330 million people in the US. That means that at least 50 million people in the United States were sexually abused as children.

Almost 50 percent of marriages end in divorce[2]. Over 30 percent of adults in the U.S. will experience an

---

[1] https://www.cdc.gov/violenceprevention/childsexualabuse/fastfact.html

[2] https://www.wf-lawyers.com/divorce-statistics-and-facts/

anxiety disorder in their lives[3], not to mention cancer, diabetes, domestic abuse, theft, poverty, recession, violence, wild fires, floods, rejection, fear, anxiety, ruptured Achilles, pulled hamstrings, car accidents, the flu, COVID, isolation, Alzheimer's, and so on.

Like I said, I'm probably a lot like you, and we all know about pain. If you are alive, you have experienced something on that list and, likely, many times. You have also experienced pain that isn't on that list. The bottom line is that none of us need a PhD to speak about pain. I have pain in my life because I am alive and human. If you are human, you are an expert.

So, as I sat in church that day, I had one of those "aha" moments. The pieces of my life experiences seemed to fall together like Tetris, and this book is my attempt to process and explain.

I'm not sure if this book is solely for my own benefit or if there is someone else out there that may find it valuable. Either way, what follows is my story, or, more accurately, my stories. It is a compilation of Tetris pieces of thoughts and experiences that lead me to the ultimate conclusions about our existence here on earth, at least in terms of pain.

While it is my story, it includes a lot of other people in my life. I didn't interview them to get their perspective. I don't claim that my tellings are exhaustive or

---

[3]   https://www.nimh.nih.gov/health/statistics/
      any-anxiety-disorder

complete, but they are how I remember things. And frankly, that is what matters here.

I've learned these lessons based on my perceptions of the events in my life. I have discovered truth by interpreting my surroundings and testing it against logic, Scripture, science, and experience. I believe this is what we are all called to do. We need to test our conclusions, and you need to test mine.

CHAPTER 1

GROWING UP IS A PAIN

I DIDN'T GROW up in a typical neighborhood. I was born in 1972 in Washington, about eighty years after it became a state. While Washington today is the home of Microsoft, Boeing, Starbucks, and Amazon, it wasn't always. Well, maybe it was for Boeing, but back in the 1970s, Washington was still essentially a wilderness state with a few cities in it. There was Seattle and a handful of other small cities, but there were mostly trees, water, mountains, and farmland.

My folks were also born and raised in Washington. They were both born in the 1940s in an even more frontier environment than I was, but by 1972, Washington had begun to mature, helped in part by the construction of I-5, which was completed in 1967.

Maybe because my dad grew up in a quickly changing Western Washington, hearing stories about

1

the Depression and of his parents coming out West, he always saw himself as a little bit of a cowboy. Maybe it was simply his exposure to Hopalong Cassidy or Bonanza and John Wayne movies. Maybe it was genetic, but to this day, my dad can still picture himself riding off into the woods on the back of a buck-colored horse with a pack and a lever action rifle. (Like all the men in my family, my dad is a little delusional.)

Regardless, two years after I was born—just outside of a small town named after a really bad transcription of a Native American word, on a street named Goat Trail Road that ran through the hills and was lined with seven or eight half-acre lots holding houses built in the 1940s—my dad found four acres of land tucked up in the woods upon which to build his homestead. (Queue the Western music.) My guess is that he couldn't find a road called the Ponderosa in that neck of the woods, so Goat Trail Road fit as good as any to establish his claim in the wilds of Mukilteo, Washington, and construct his ranch with his own two hands—the way God intended! And so he did.

Was he prepared? No. Experienced? Nope. Cash rich? Not even close. At the time, my dad was a public school history teacher and football coach, and my mom stayed at home with me and my older brother and sister. He had never built a house before, but neither had the settlers, and they figured it out. So, he bought an axe to clear a driveway, a book on how to build houses, and a seventeen-foot trailer for the five of us to live in. I'm sure my mother was ecstatic. What more could a woman want than to live in a trailer in the woods for a couple years with her three kids while helping her husband build a house? Paradise! (She's lucky it wasn't a covered wagon.) But build it he did, and it became the house I grew up in.

Out back, we had a pasture with a pond in it. We had trails through the woods that led to seemingly endless exploration. We built a barn, then tried to fill it. We went through multiple dogs and cats. We had a horse and a pony for a few of those. We had chickens (from the guy up the road who, unfortunately for him, still lived within the city limits, and his neighbor complained of their early morning clucking). And at one point, we even had a cow, which came to us as partial payment for work my dad had completed.

I've got to hand it to him. My dad had a dream, and he made it happen. In the middle of what grew up into the picture of American suburbs, I grew up on a homestead in the woods, building forts, exploring the forest, trapping frogs, and building houses in the summer with my dad. As I look back on my childhood, we seem a bit like characters in a turn-of-the century American novel. We didn't have much besides our land and our family. We just made do.

My dad turned house-building into a business because he had to. We were a family of five living on a single public-school teacher's salary. We had very little money, but my parents did what was needed to get by. My dad worked a lot. My mom baked, cooked, and sewed. We did not go out to eat. We shopped at the outlet stores (did I mention that once we got paid in cow?), and we absolutely did not get whatever the latest thing was that all the other kids had. My parents rarely said we couldn't afford things. They would just say, "It's a fad," and that was enough for them. Fashion, toys, music playing devices—the latest versions would all fade into the next latest versions, and the expenditure could not be justified when we needed to spend the money on more permanent things.

So, at no point in our childhood were any of us fashionable. We didn't have the cool things or the cool toys. We were different. I think my brother and sister were more aware of this than I was, but even for me, there was always an embarrassment of being just slightly "off". My clothes kind of looked similar to the other kids, but they were off brands or homemade, so any close look made it clear they weren't quite right. While I liked my life on the hill in the woods, those moments at school when I would be reminded of what we lacked were embarrassing. So, besides my mother's skill at the sewing machine, we tried to stay somewhat up-to-date with fashion.

One of those ways was our annual, close of the school year, shopping spree where we would go catch up on the latest styles. Typically, they were the previous year's fashions, but to us, they were gold. We would go to the high school lost-and-found before it was all thrown out and scrounge through the bins for clothes and shoes that might fit. Most people left behind better things than we could afford, so it was something I looked forward to. I never made the connection that other people didn't do this. Instead, I felt like Indiana Jones searching through the bins for potential buried treasure, and every now and then, I would hit the jackpot with a fake leather jacket, Adidas-striped running shorts, or brand-named jeans. Mostly though, just like my archaeologist colleagues, it was an exercise in frustration; the wrong size, a tear in the sleeve, or a smell.

The shoes were the most frustrating. Shoes were expensive, so we never spent money on cool shoes. Our one shot at Nike or Adidas was our annual foray into the lost-and-found. You don't know frustration until you find a Nike running shoe that fits... that's right, a shoe. Nobody loses a *pair* of shoes.

Our family clearly didn't have much money, but my parents made sure that didn't extend to my siblings and me. It was very important to them that we understand the nature of work and the value of money, so the irony was that while my family didn't have much, I always had enough. Unlike my wealthier friends, from the time I was nine or ten, I would work all summer with my brother and dad and get paid for it. It didn't really change any of my outward appearance. I still wasn't allowed to spend it on "fads," but I regularly walked down to the store with my friends and bought candy or went to the movies or "walked the mall" (such an 80's thing to do). I was probably a bit more frugal than they were, but I was still able to do it. Later, I realized that while I was spending my own money, they were buying candy with money their parents had given them from something called an "allowance."

Working all summer was hard, and I knew that money was not something to be wasted. So, I grew up having money but never being comfortable with it. I'm sure my parents wished there was more money, but it wasn't a thing that we really discussed. Money was scarce and had to be managed, so we didn't blow it on what my dad would call "frills." Call me naïve, but I wasn't aware that we were "going without." It seemed like we had lots: land, animals, clothes, family. The hard part wasn't so much that I had less. It was that what I had was different, and different is hard. Different stands out. Even different that is good sets you apart. It makes you feel alone, and alone hurts.

One of the ways that we stood out is that we didn't have cable or a decent TV, for that matter. I remember staying home from church to watch the 1980 gold medal hockey game on TV. This was a really big moment for me as a kid, and it only had a small part to do with the hockey team and game. Our family didn't miss church for anything, and we weren't hockey fans. We didn't even watch the Olympics much, but we stayed home from church that day, and that made me sit up and take notice.

Forty years later, I clearly remember the game against Finland. I can picture that "miracle on ice" being played out on our little twenty-something-inch TV after we turned the channel with a pair of pliers and fiddled with the rabbit-ear antennas. Fortunately, sports were still broadcast on network TV because ABC, NBC, and CBS were three of the five or six stations we could get (counting PBS, which really shouldn't count, and CBS didn't come in very well). I remember both the specialness of the moment in sports history and the specialness in our family history, but I also remember how pathetic our TV was.

Once, a friend of my brother came over and said, "I didn't know this show was ever in black and white!" to which my mom replied, "All shows are in black and white here—It's the TV, not the show." Mortifying.

I understand that TV may sound like a trivial thing, but growing up in the 1980s without cable set us apart. We didn't have ESPN or MTV. These two new broadcasting companies were my generation's contribution to the world. The Greatest Generation saved the world from the Nazis. Baby Boomers brought civil rights and fought valiantly against the spread of Communism. My generation? We produced distraction: drugs, money, music, and TV. We elevated entertainment to a level never seen before in human history. The gateway drugs to the entertainment frontier were ESPN and MTV, and I didn't have either one.

We knew about these channels. We were aware. We just didn't experience them. I remember trying to get reception to some Canadian channel because it played music videos once a week for thirty minutes. I just hoped they would show at least a couple of videos that my friends were talking about, but when you were limited to maybe five or six videos per week, and at least one of them was John Cougar Melencamp (I guess Canadians loved John Cougar), the odds of seeing the coolest new music video diminished quite a bit.

Cable TV wasn't the only critical measure of status that we missed out on though. As our lost-and-found forays would indicate, my brother, sister, and I did not participate in the heights of fashion. Fashion is very important to teens of all generations, but this was especially true in the 1980s. From bell-bottoms to skinny ties to parachute pants, the 80s covered a fashion spectrum that was nearly unrecognizable from the beginning to the end of the decade. There was even that weird phase where girls wore blouses with long skirts as if they just stepped off the set as an extra on *Little House on the Prairie*. The look was usually capped off with a huge pair of glasses with big round frames ingeniously connected at the bottom of the lens instead of the traditional top. What was that all about? Anyway, fashion was important, and as I've mentioned, my mom sewed my clothes.

I made the most of it, though. My clothes were never "in," but I had other qualities that kept me from being ostracized for my off-brand jeans. I was a good student, an athlete, funny, and I was a boy. Unfortunately, it was much harder for my sister for no other reason than she was a girl—same qualities but not the same benefits. Life isn't fair.

But it wasn't just TV and clothes. We never went out to eat either, and that included McDonald's. I remember going to stay at a friend's house one summer. It was in Eastern Washington, and it was hot. I have vivid memories from that trip. They had cable! I found ESPN boring, but I watched it anyway, so I knew what it was. They had He-Man action figures too. I can clearly picture sitting in the basement playing with Ram-Man with his springy legs and shooting missiles out of Battle Cat's harness. (This was before the lawyers got ahold of everything and ruined toys forever.)

I also remember going with them to the water slides — waterslides were big in the 80s. This seemed a crazy extravagance for me. There was no way we would ever spend money to careen down hill on a big slide into a pool, not when my dad could just turn on the hose in the backyard. We could slide through the grass and mud any time we liked, and there were only a few scratches and bruises from the rocks in the ground. Just as good, right?

The biggest impression from that trip though, came from a stop we made before heading to the slides: McDonald's. As I said, my family almost never went out to eat. We packed sandwiches or ate at home, but we didn't waste precious money eating something we (my mother) could cook ourselves (herself). We just didn't spend money that way. So, I was astounded when these people just drove up to a restaurant and threw money out the window like oil tycoons, and food popped into the car. (That was when I knew the Communists didn't have a chance.)

When I realized that these people were buying me food as well, and they clearly were wealthy beyond belief — they had cable, for criminy sakes! — I knew I needed to make it count. So, when they asked me what I wanted, I made sure I didn't look like a newbie, and I ordered the only thing I knew was on the menu: a Big Mac. I was so excited. This had to be the best burger in the world! They had even composed a song about it... two all-beef patties, special sauce, lettuce, cheese... The anticipation hung heavily in the air. It may have been the longest four-and-a-half-minute wait in my life.

The bag was finally handed through the window. My friend's mother sorted through the bag like she had done it before. She was clearly a pro. She reached in and passed out food to each person in the car until she finally gave me a yellow, Styrofoam box that promised to be the pinnacle of my culinary life.

My hands tremored as I opened that treasure chest of deliciousness. And I was horrified. It had all this "stuff" on it; pickles, onions, lettuce, and sauce. I had never really thought about the song. That was definitely a mistake, because now I had squandered my brief visit into the world of the rich and famous, but more importantly, I realized someone had ruined this burger! I was embarrassed. I was disappointed. I was hungry, but I didn't think I could get it down, so I left it in the car.

I ate my fries (which didn't disappoint at all), and we went to the waterslides. They were amazing. I didn't get a single cut on my stomach from a stray pebble. I slid and jumped out and ran back up to get in line over and over and over again. So, when we came back to the car a couple of hours later, I was hungry enough to choke down anything — even the falsely-advertised, bastardized hamburger that had stolen my innocence earlier that morning.

Thankfully, hours later, it was still hot. While we spent the day at the slides, the burger had been warming under the rear window in the ninety-degree heat of Eastern Washington. It was like the best heat lamp ever created. Looking back, I was probably lucky I didn't get sick with the bacteria-growing machine that was three-hour, solar-heated special sauce. I absolutely devoured that Big Mac, shoving the last couple bites in quickly as my friend's mother tried to stop me from poisoning myself, and my eyes were forever opened to McDonald's world of decadent delights. To this day, I can trace a straight line from that moment to about twenty pounds of the extra weight I still carry now.

That was my childhood. We were oddly different, and uniquely rich. On the whole, I loved it, but that perspective comes with time. In the midst of it, many times, growing up was just hard.

I loved my parents. I was fortunate to live in a house my dad literally built with his own two hands. I was fortunate to have a mom that loved me, spent time with me, cut my hair, sewed my clothes, and made my food. But despite the foundational blessings we enjoyed, when the outside world intruded, embarrassment was a constant companion. Our clothes weren't quite right, our lunches weren't the same, and we didn't see or listen to the same things. We just didn't have the *stuff* my friends had. The funny thing was that I didn't connect what we lacked with not being *able* to have that stuff. I assumed my parents were just driven by their principles. "Money is hard to come by. We don't waste it on frivolous things like TV," and, to be honest, that made me mad.

I liked my home and family, but I didn't want to have my friends over and suggest we catch frogs, explore the woods, or play pretend. And what else were we going to do? As an adult, I know it sounds silly. My friends would probably have loved all of that, but like most kids, I operated out of fear. I just didn't want to be embarrassed by our TV.

That's the key point in this for me: "like most kids, I operated out of fear." Some might look at my child-hood and focus on my intact family and my home in the woods and my experiences exploring and building and say how lucky I was. They would be right. Others might look at the things that I lacked. They might point to our forays into the lost-and-found bins and the images of the poor kids in the woods and feel pity for the ridicule that we experienced and the shame that went along with it. They would be right too.

I would say that I was really, really lucky to have the family and the situation I had. I would say that no lack of material wealth can really overshadow a loving and supportive family. I would say that, in some ways, my childhood was very different than most. Some of those ways were good and some of those ways were bad. Unfortunately, many children do not experience the safety and love that I grew up with. Many children also do not grow up dreading the approach of summer vacation because it meant long hours of working con-struction in the hot sun.

I would also say that in other ways my childhood was very typical. I went to school and I played sports and I played with my friends all the while learning to cope with fear and shame and anxiety and depres-sion. It was just like others in that it was painful. My experiences may not have been like everyone else's experiences, but what is true for everyone is that growing up hurts. Sometimes it is abuse. Sometimes it is abandonment. Sometimes it is shame or embarrassment. But no one escapes childhood unscathed.

I do not claim to have a traumatic childhood as compared to some. That is the point. My pain may not be like your pain, but it was real. I really did experience hurt. You experienced hurt. Everyone does. The embarrassment of my clothes or TV, the fear of not fitting in, the shame of being different, these things all hurt, and explaining it away doesn't really make it go away.

It wasn't till I accepted this and stopped pretending that my pain wasn't real because it didn't compare to the tragedies depicted on After School Specials, that I finally started to heal.

CHAPTER 2

WHAT IS PAIN?

I GREW UP in a big house on a hill surrounded by trees and pasture, looking out over the Puget Sound with the sun setting over the Olympic Mountains on what would later become one of the wealthier areas in my little section of the world. I worked all summer, took care of the animals, played in the woods, dug through the lost-and-found bins, and fiddled with rabbit ears with a wrench to watch TV. My parents stayed together. They loved each other, and they loved us. They provided and served and disciplined. As many of my friends' parents divorced, mine didn't. They were active in their love toward each other. They did things together and took care of each other. They fought and argued, but they laughed together too.

Looking back, we had so much! It's funny how much you can take things for granted. I was incredibly fortunate, but at the time, it was hard not to focus on what we didn't have: TV, clothes, cars... things. We were normal kids. We wanted all those things, all the *stuff*, but they just weren't options for us. Things cost money, and money was something we simply didn't have much of. It was embarrassing, and I couldn't change it. Even though I knew what we had was more important than what we didn't, I also knew that despite everything I had, I was in danger of being labeled as "poor."

I have never liked that word. Poor is what people with more call people with less. I never thought we were poor. (I think most poor people feel the same way.)

That isn't to say that I wasn't aware that other people had more money than we did. We clearly had less, so in the economic sense of the word, we were poor. We lived in the woods. You might even say we were borderline redneck, but "poor" isn't the right word. People use the word poor to mean something concrete and definable. If you are below this income or wealth level, if you don't have enough, you are poor, but that isn't correct. Poor isn't a concrete term. It's relative. Poor always means "compared to others."

How dumb is that? Literally everyone is poor in comparison to someone else, and the only people that balk at the relative nature of being poor are those who don't want to be called poor because they can see so many poor people below them. Someone always has more. Someone always has something of value that someone else lacks.

Regardless of whether I could articulate this as a child, it became clear to me that labeling me as poor was passing judgment on what I valued. They were saying I was somehow disadvantaged. I was somehow hand-icapped in life. They were saying I was less able unless those with cable TV helped me out. That made me angry.

It also made me sad. I did not want to be judged by the things I did not have. I am not the sum of my defi-ciencies. I have talents and skills and qualities that are a much better judge of my value than what I may lack compared to someone else. Despite the challenges, I felt like I had a lot, and it seemed unfair to be pre-judged based on things that didn't seem all that important to me in the first place. Being laughed at, or worse, being pitied hurt, and I did not want that pain. So, early on, I made a decision. I decided I would take control of what I could and wouldn't allow circumstances I couldn't do anything about control me. I learned I could impact the way others perceived me. If I was embarrassed, I was a victim. If I was confident, it was a choice. My attitude made all the difference.

The kid wearing thrift store clothes because she is a non-conforming free spirit and the one doing the same thing because he has no other choice are virtually dressed in the same way. From a physical and visual standpoint, they are the same. Yet the perception of these two people are as far apart as can be. No one feels sorry for the thrift store girl, at least not for her clothes. She chooses to dress that way. Her circumstances are not thrust upon her. She thrusts herself into her circumstances.

Internally and externally, the one who owns his circumstances and lives in them and through them no longer inspires pity or derision but respect and sometimes admiration or even jealousy. By owning her circumstances, the thrift store girl no longer feels persecuted or put upon, but her inherent value transcends the trappings of the material world; choice, attitude – all the difference. At least that's the theory.

It sounds pretty deep, and I'd like to say I acquired this perspective from something like the Bible, a pastor, or an inspirational book, but I think it pretty much came from my dad (and maybe a little from watching our pathetic little television). My dad, the modern-day frontiersman, used to love telling us stories of Roger Banister breaking the four-minute mile and soldiers surviving the Bataan Death March. He had played college football for the University of Washington in the 1960s, and when we could wheedle the stories out of him, he would also tell us about the blatantly abusive practices he would endure. Football was a different sport back then. Among many other things, they would run until they literally dropped. The coaches would tell them to start running and you weren't done until you were actually physically done. If you quit too early, it told the coaches what they needed to know. Contrary to the expectations of our current victimhood culture, my dad never told those stories with an edge of bitterness or regret. Instead, there was a bit of pride underlying each telling of the story; pride in outlasting the hardship (Hardship. Pain. Pride. Go figure).

Whether it was Roger Banister, WWII, or 1960s collegiate football, the message was the same each time: mind over matter. Your body will tell you to quit, but you can always do more. You will be tempted to stop because you do not want to experience pain. You will want to avoid the shame of failure. You will want to avoid exhaustion. You will want to tell yourself that you have reached your limit, but you can always go further. Pain is relative.

So, I learned early that what I let limit me was largely my choice. I learned to struggle with internal or emotional pain. I suppressed feelings like shame, disappointment, and embarrassment because if I let those things show, I invited a whole new kind of pain from ridicule, pity, animosity, or bullying.

My circumstances may have placed me in a family with less money, but I would own those circumstances. I wasn't poor. I was strong. I wasn't one of those soft kids that had everything given to them. I worked. I endured. I earned. Turned out, converting pain to strength was just a trick of the mind. The more I did it, the easier it got, kind of. Pain may be relative, but it is never easy.

This is probably why I don't like to speak about my pain. It admits weakness, and furthermore, it feels like I'm participating in the same relative judgment as those who would have called me poor. Speaking aloud about my pain felt like I was volunteering to compare mine with others', and there is always something worse than what you are experiencing. Someone has always endured more. Every time I stubbed a toe or scraped a knee, I was reminded of Rocky Balboa fighting with his eyes swollen shut, yelling, "Cut me, Mick!" I thought of stories of Junior Coffee playing football for the University of Washington on a broken foot. I thought of the soldiers in WWII that marched from Bataan. And because I grew up in a Christian home, there was always the knowledge that Jesus Christ died an excruciating death on a cross. Who was I to complain? My pain was nothing.

But that's a lie. My pain wasn't nothing. No matter how much I denied it, no matter how much I shifted my perspective, I couldn't make it go away. I could push through it. I could survive it, but I couldn't make myself not feel it. The problem with mind over matter, is that matter exists and no matter how much perspective you gain, no matter how small it becomes in relation to something else, you can never make it disappear. Pain is real. Case in point: You know your pain is real when you are eight years old, messing around with a stapler, and you staple your index finger. Am I the only one who has done that?

I really don't remember a lot about the build-up to my stapler incident. I do remember the motivation, though. There is something satisfying about the way a stapler works, the way the staples cleanly push through pieces of paper, and the tension and the release as the leverage overcomes the glue holding the staples together. I don't know exactly what it is, but it is somehow akin to popping a zit. Pressure, pressure, release (don't judge me).

So, I was playing around with a stapler, and, of course, I wanted to feel the staple come out, because that was the whole reason I was playing with it. I gripped my hand around the mechanism with my fingers in between the stapler section and the base. I wanted to squeeze the magazine that held the staples up into the top of the stapler so I could witness with the touch of a finger the moment at which the staples gave way. I reached my hand around and gently applied pressure so it would happen slowly. I squeezed, and... Nothing happened.

The problem was that to experience a controlled result like the one I was aiming for, you needed enough strength to control the output, and my eight-year-old hands weren't strong enough to produce a slowly controlled squeeze to break free the staple from its glue.

Another thing I have learned about myself is that I have a tendency to focus so much on solving the problem in front of me that I sometimes forget the context of the problem. I will see the obstacle, and my attention goes to solely overcoming that obstacle. This tendency has served me well over the years. That focus has been incredibly effective in many areas of my life, but it also leaves me open to tunnel vision, like when my laser focus was on getting that staple out.

So, I re-gripped and tried again. I used two hands this time and readjusted my fingers to apply more leverage. I carefully placed my right index finger over the slot where the staple comes out so I could feel it as it poked through. I squeezed gently but firmly. Nothing. I squeezed a bit harder. Nothing. I squeezed a bit... All at once, the staple gave way. There was nothing gradual about it; right through the tip of my finger and up against the underside of my fingernail. I remember the shock of pulling my finger out and looking at it. There was a little metallic line running parallel to the under-side of my finger. I turned it over and saw a little pin-point circle showing through my fingernail that I knew was one of the staple's prongs. It didn't even hurt. At least not yet. I grabbed the staple with the fingertips of my left hand and pulled it out like a knife out of a butcher block, leaving only two little pinpricks of blood. Then, of course, came the pain. In case you are worried, I survived. I kept the finger.

I think this is where I began to learn another lesson: You can't describe pain. I had shoved a needle-like projectile into the nerve cluster of a fingertip until it pressed against the underside of my fingernail. The pain was shocking. But what came out of my mouth as I ran to my mother, shaking my finger and waving it around, screaming, and crying was "Mom! Moooommmm!"

"What's wrong? Calm down. Tell me what happened."

"I stapled my finger."

If you are a parent, you know my mom's struggle in this moment. You know all the warring emotions and thoughts: *Oh my! That's gotta hurt. Phew! It's not serious. Is there something wrong with my son? What kind of idiot staples his finger?!*

Here I was experiencing the worst pain possible in the world—from my perspective anyway—and the look on my mother's face wasn't what I expected. It wasn't what I needed it to be. It wasn't the acceptable reaction a mother should have in the face of unspeakable tragedy. She didn't drop to her knees and hold me while calling 9-1-1 and extolling the injustice of our fallen world. She looked... puzzled. That's when I started wrestling with the nature of pain. I had stapled my finger. I didn't die on a cross.

How could I say I was experiencing real pain? Others had gone through so much more. Complaining and crying about my physical pain resulted in the same outcome as showing emotional pain: ridicule, pity, animosity, or bullying.

Maybe that's why I've always struggled with going to the doctor, and they ask you to rate your pain on a scale from one to ten. Inside, I know my head is pounding, my throat hurts, and I feel miserable. But I'm being asked to put a numerical value on my pain like it is an objective thing. That is so much harder. If one is no pain and ten is the worst pain you can have, then ten is something like being burned alive. I'm nowhere close to that. I'm probably a four or five. But if I say four or five, I'm not getting the relief that I came here for from my very real pain. The nurse will look at me with that puzzled look that my mom had. "Why are you wasting my time with a five?"

I struggled with this for years. When I was in my 30s, I saw a Brian Regan standup comedy bit about it. It was spot on. He absolutely nailed it. I laughed until I cried and couldn't breathe. You ever laugh so hard that you don't get enough oxygen, and your head kind of goes fuzzy and hurts? It's about a five.

While we are on the topic of pain and against my better judgment, let me admit that childbirth makes no sense to me either. When I went to the child birthing classes as a soon-to-be father, and they described a process that I simply couldn't reconcile with anything a sane person would voluntarily experience, I looked at my wife, thinking, *That has to be at least an eight*, and inexplicably, she says to me, "I really want to do this naturally."

I thought, *Huh?! She can't mean what I think that means. Maybe there is some kind of organic, "natural" anesthetic she wants to use. She can't mean that she wants to feel this! If they would have allowed it, I would have taken an epidural for my last sinus infection, and she wants to squeeze out a watermelon and feel the whole thing? What is wrong with her?! She wants me to participate in this disfunction? Honey, do you really think special breathing is going to help this? Special breathing?! You are nuts, lady! The only way any breathing technique will help this is if you hold your breath till you pass out.*

But by that time in my life I knew better than to voice all those thoughts, so I tactfully and sensitively said, "Are you sure you want to do that?" At least it seemed tactful and sensitive to me. I guess it didn't to her. I don't need to replay the entire fight that ensued, but the highlights were:

Kari: Millions of women for thousands of years have experienced natural childbirth. I can handle it.

Joel: Millions of men for thousands of years have experienced compound fractures. What does history have to do with it, and why would you *want* to handle it?

Kari: I want to be fully present.

Joel: Why in the world would you want to be fully present for *that*?!

Kari: Childbirth is a miraculous and beautiful experience.

Joel: I'm not sure you were paying attention in class.

Ultimately through theses experiences, there are two things I have learned about the nature of pain. The first is that pain is both concrete and relative. It is a concrete, real, and very much personal and individual thing. It concretely exists, but pain is also relative. It is not, however, relative in the way most people describe it. It is not relative to other people's pain. It is relative to your own. The amount you feel is relative to the amount you have experienced. The severity is relative to your own experience. It is also relative in your ability to communicate your pain to someone else, because just as your perception of pain is relative to your experience, their understanding of your pain is relative to their experience.

I grew up in a loving and supportive home. Compared to almost all of my friends and frankly, the vast majority of the entire world, I had it really, really good, but I still grew up with a lot of internal pain. Explaining other's circumstances or rationalizing it did not make it go away. Outside of some typical, negative experiences, the pain of my childhood was surface and material, and it was very real.

Like everyone on earth, I experienced pain on a daily basis. There were times when I shrugged it off and times when I cried so hard I thought I would throw up. We all grow up this way. The circumstances are irrelevant.

Tell a thirteen-year-old she is grounded from Instagram. Watch a grown man react to stubbing his toe. Send a little boy to school in homemade corduroy pants. Now rate that pain on a scale from one to ten. In the moment, those are all tens, not in retrospect, not in comparison to some historic event; in the moment. They may not be tens as compared to the atrocities that the world can produce. In real time, though, they are all tens.

It is only in retrospect that we assign a scale to pain. It is only after we stop feeling it that we start to compare. As we reflect on those experiences, watch our children process them, and as we step back from the embarrassment of screaming and jumping around on one foot, we rationally place those instances back into a comparative order of the pain scale.

Even then we don't do this on an absolute basis though. I can only rate my pain compared to my knowledge of pain. Because stubbing my toe is really and truly painful, I can only assign it a lower number if I have witnessed or have knowledge of more severe pain. My experience provides context to pain. Others simply cannot understand my personal pain without their own context to which they compare it.

This shows up in one of my favorite pastimes which brings me back to the subject of childbirth. I love to watch men as women discuss this. Nine months of nausea, back pain, and the rearranging of bones and internal organs culminates with a procedure that, if not associated with the bringing of life, would only belong in a 1980s horror movie. Men listen to this being described and invariably find themselves in one of three camps.

There is the Miracle of Life/Strength of Women Everywhere camp. These men hope to ingratiate themselves into the club of femininity by exalting womanhood and debasing themselves. Sorry, dude. This never works.

Then there is the I Can Relate/I Have Pain Too camp. These men hope to be included by illustrating that they have an understanding of what it is like to go through pain as well (not sure why "Well you've never been kicked in the balls" always enters the conversation here). This is usually well-intentioned but foolish and always, ultimately, a failure. Fellas, you will never be validated by comparing passing a kidney stone to pushing a cantaloupe out of a garden hose.

Lastly, there is the Sit Quietly/Don't Make Eye Contact camp. These men have learned the futility of trying to belong to the club. They only hope to avoid drawing attention to themselves as there is always one woman who will connect the you-did-that-to-me dots while waiting for the conversation to move back to more easily navigable topics, like religion or politics. The masters of this camp wait for an opportune moment, grab a beer, and slip away to talk about football until the conversation is over.

If you find yourself in camps one or two, understand that there is only life in camp three. Because men will never have the shared experience or potential shared experience of childbirth, women know that they can never understand it. Pain is relative to one's experience.

The second thing I know about pain is that it is both physical and emotional. Small pain is usually called discomfort or anxiety. Large pain is called agony or trauma. Sometimes it is called trouble, trials, diet, exercise, or family reunions... but it is all pain.

While you can conceivably experience emotional pain without physical pain, I don't think you can experience physical pain without the emotional. Physical pain is inextricably linked to emotional pain. Falling and scraping my knee, scrubbing the infection on my knee, or someone holding me down and taking sandpaper to my knee are basically all the same types of physical pain. But the emotions and psychology that are associated with each make the sandpaper horrifying and unbearable.

I think we all understand this, but conversations around pain seem to center only around the physical aspects. Maybe this is because pain is such an unspecific word, kind of like love. Its meaning is something to which we all agree but also has many underlying meanings. My love for my wife and my love of football are not the same thing (they are really close, but there are nuances). The pain I feel from the loss of a loved one and the pain I felt when I watched the movie *About*

Time—great movie—are both pain. I really do feel pain in both instances.

Maybe pain is also attached to pride. Pain is like the overarching category in which we place all forms of discomfort, but at the same time, the word itself has weight. I don't want to admit that it hurts when some moron at my kid's soccer game shouts out the score of the Seahawks game I am recording at home. I was really looking forward to hanging out for a couple hours and having a beer and some snacks while watching football. The game wasn't that important, but the loss of the experience was. Even further, I don't want to admit the devastation I feel over the loss of a pet until, of course, I know it is safe to do so. I rationalize, compare, and explain to myself, but really, it just hurts. And I know it doesn't hurt at the same level as losing a spouse, but it really, really hurts. I would rather break an arm than lose my dog. Both are pain, but sometimes there is shame in admitting emotional or psychological pain. In many ways, feeling pain is more acceptable when stubbing a toe than with depression. But anyone who has experienced the pain of depression will take the toe.

I think the actual reason why we tend to downplay emotional pain is that it is the pain we cannot bear. It is too threatening. We talk about the horrible things in the world: murder, rape, and cancer, but we use these outward labels so we don't have to discuss what truly makes these things hurtful: loss, violation, impotence, isolation, fear.

This is why I think I reflect upon my childhood in a positive way. I was poor, lived in the woods, and didn't have much. In describing many of the things I experienced, people often genuinely exclaim surprise that I turned out even as relatively normal as I have. Some would say my experiences bordered on abuse, child labor, and neglect. I didn't see it that way then, and I don't now.

First, I was unaware of my relative poverty. I knew I didn't have as much as others, but I didn't understand the breadth of the gap between us. As I explained earlier, I didn't think I was poor, I just was. I simply didn't have context to assign pain to what I lacked.

Second, and I think this is much more important, my delusional father and my Susie Homemaker mother loved each other, and they loved me. In the midst of spankings, hardships, and going without, I never associated our material shortages with malice. I knew that what they withheld from me, they withheld out of love. They believed it was for the best. I knew I worked in the summers while my friends played because we needed to provide for the family, and my father believed it was good for me to learn how to work. I knew he didn't see it as depriving me but as the opposite. He was providing me valuable lessons and experiences.

Don't get me wrong here. I didn't like it. I was mad many times. I was hurt. I was frustrated. But the pain of my childhood didn't linger. It never settled on the inside.

I think if I had to go into a doctor's office and describe my childhood in clinical terms, professionals might rate it as a six or seven. However, that is just them assigning significance to my experiences based on their context and understanding. I would rate it as a two or three because I was fortunate enough to be ignorant of what I went without and because of the love of my parents; most of that pain never landed in an emotional sense.

It really wasn't till later in my life when I would tell stories of my childhood to people that I started to question my conclusions. I would tell stories that I thought were funny and, invariably, the reactions would be laughter and horror. Some people would laugh, but there was always one or two of the more empathetic in the crowd that would look at me with sad eyes like they knew I was just coping by making light of my pain.

I was. I absolutely make light of it, just like I make light of dropping a hammer on my foot. I do it later. Pain is only funny when the person is not permanently or seriously hurt. Then it is hilarious, and I never felt my pain was serious or permanent until people questioned it.

Then I started digging, and I learned a lot. I learned that, for the most part, they were wrong. I was fine. I laughed about the painful memories because I was not hurt by them. However, I also learned that in some things, they were right. There was pain that I didn't share. There was pain that the empaths didn't even know I had buried. That worried me a bit. I needed to understand how this pain thing worked. How could they, and I, both be so wrong at the same time?

Eventually, I figured out exactly what I have already mentioned. The reason they didn't understand my pain and the reason they knew I had pain I wasn't acknowledging is that everyone has pain, and pain is not defined by your circumstances but by the context, meaning, and emotion associated with those circumstances.

Pain is personal and relative, and always feels like a ten in the moment. The scale is meaningless. There is no external, absolute measure for pain.

Our hurts are on the inside. Our pain is carried within, and the pain we bury is the pain that will eventually bury us.

CHAPTER 3

NO PAIN, NO GAIN

SEVERAL MORE INTELLIGENT people than I have written on the topic of why pain exists. My personal favorite is C. S. Lewis in his *Problem of Pain*[4]. Admittedly, it is a pretty difficult book to get through. It probably needs a *Problem of Pain for Dummies,* or Eugene Peterson needs to write a Message version, but if you can wade through it, it is outstanding. So, if you would like to delve into the metaphysical aspects of the existence of pain, especially where it seemingly conflicts with the existence of a loving God, I would point you in that direction.

For the purposes of this book, though, I don't have any interest in trying to convince anyone as to the *why* behind pain. Frankly, I think there is enough to talk about regarding the *what*.

---

[4] Lewis, C.S.. *The Problem of Pain*. New York: Macmilan, 1962.

Pain exists. Whether or not I want it to be true, think it should be true, or God should have allowed it, it is. Pain exists. The issue we need to address is not "why" or "what if" but how to deal with it, and to do that, we have to start disabusing ourselves of the lies we believe about pain.

I dealt with the first lie already. Pain is not some external factor on an absolute scale. Pain is relative, personal, and internal. The way we deal with pain is completely in context as to our experience, attitude, resources, and outlook. My childhood could easily have produced significantly more pain in my life than it did. What can I say? It just didn't. My poverty didn't scar me. I didn't allow my differentness to set me apart. I had security in my family and self-worth that shielded me from degrees of pain that many others experience.

That doesn't mean that other people are inventing their pain. It is real. I know when my child cries, he does so out of genuine hurt. Regardless of whether or not I would experience the same level of hurt given the same circumstances, his pain exists, and he feels it. It is real and personal to him.

This first lie causes us to deny the pain in our lives rather than deal with it. The second one causes us to avoid it all together. This lie has to do with this generic bucket that we put pain in: the bad bucket. Pain is bad. That is a lie.

Pain is not bad. We may not like it, but it is incredibly useful (insert sound or needle scratching across record player). What?! Hold on, Leroy! How in the Sam Heck is pain useful?!

As I have made abundantly clear, I grew up in the 1970s and 80s. I'm sure most people feel the same way about the time in which they grew into adulthood, but this was a very interesting time to be alive. In the 70s, the Vietnam War ended, Elvis died, Nixon was impeached (our country actually used to get outraged by elected officials leveraging governmental power to influence elections), interest rates went up to nearly 20 percent, energy shortages arose, Islamic terrorists entered the scene, the Cold War was in full bloom, and hippies had been replaced by Yuppies, disco dancers, and punk rockers. Then, as we entered the 1980s, America embraced body image.

Action movies weren't invented in the 80s, but they certainly evolved and took center stage during the decade. Stars like Charles Bronson and Clint Eastwood faded while Arnold Schwarzenegger and Sylvester Stallone dominated the genre: *Conan the Barbarian, Conan the Destroyer, Terminator, Commando, Predator, First Blood, Rambo: First Blood Part II, Rambo III, Rocky III*, and *Rocky IV* (Sylvester Stallone never met a sequel he didn't like).

Throughout all these movies, the action stars evolved. Just take a look at how Rocky's body changes through the movies to reflect how body image changed at the same time. Rocky Balboa transformed over the years from the flabby kid from Philly in *Rocky* to a chiseled, oiled-down Chippendale's dancer, seducing the polit-buro and shifting the political thinking of the Eastern Bloc in *Rocky IV*. Professional wrestling gained in popularity, especially as the wrestlers themselves began to look more like body builders than the brawlers of the decades before. Aerobics classes and video tapes were so popular that leotards and leg warmers became everyday fashion. Jane Fonda enjoyed more success starring in her workout videos than she did in her acting career. Steroids and plastic surgery surged into the mainstream.

During this era, everyone knew the phrase, "No pain, no gain." Since that time, this saying has lost its luster as those who feel obliged to keep watch over society lest we hurt ourselves have decried the saying as contributing to exercise-based injury (there is no place in a civilized world for muscle strains!). These people made it known that pain and injury were linked, to which the vast majority of us responded, "Did you really think we didn't know that?"

We all know that pain is no fun. It is unpleasant. It hurts. It's... painful. But as our society progressed away from the excess of the 80s and into the positive reinforcement and participation trophies of the 90s, we lost sight that there *was actually* no gain without pain.

That isn't to say that all pain creates gain. That would be a fallacy in logic. Something can be inherently useful and essential without every application of it being positive. Water is necessary for life. That doesn't mean we can't drown in it.

No one is claiming that the existence of pain isn't correlated with the risk of injury. Pain is absolutely linked to the potential for harm because pain is a warning. "Don't touch that!" "Don't go there!" There is nothing pleasant about a smoke alarm, an air raid siren, or a mother yelling, "Get that out of your mouth!" Warnings aren't pleasant, but that doesn't make them bad. Warnings are useful. They keep us safe, and they let us know and test boundaries.

Of course, nobody likes pain in and of itself. Sharp needles, hot stoves, fire, bees, nettles, sliding into second base wearing shorts... If we can, we avoid it unless, of course, you are knee-deep in the afore-mentioned natural childbirth dilemma. Come to think of it, there are many other examples besides childbirth: belly flops, stretching, spicy food, contact sports, popping a pimple, CrossFit...

In fact, the evidence would indicate that we don't avoid pain. Many of us seek it out on a daily basis. We call it challenge, discipline, confrontation, thrill-seeking, or competition. Maybe pain lets us know we are alive. Maybe we want to know we have overcome or conquered something—"That jalapeño has nothing on me." Maybe it is cathartic—it feels like we are purging weakness or sickness from our bodies. Maybe it is because we know consciously, subconsciously, and instinctually that pain is necessary for growth, for life—without pain in my life, I fear I am dying.

Just because pain and injury are linked doesn't mean that pain isn't linked to anything else. If you push too far through that pain, you can definitely harm yourself, but at the same time, anyone who has experienced growth in his life has also experienced pain. Pain is necessary for growth and is the ultimate "rock and a hard place." Yes, too much pain causes injury, inhibits growth, and can result in stagnation or regression. But also, the absence of pain creates the same result: stagnation, degeneration, and decay. There's the catch. Nobody likes pain, but dude! No pain, no gain (aah! The wisdom of the 80s).

What we really do is rather than avoid pain, we evaluate the pain in our lives constantly; what is the purpose, intensity, duration, outcome, or some combination of it all? Assuming we have a choice in the matter, the deciding factor on whether or not we are willing to endure pain in the circumstances of our lives is context; it is the perception of the outcome of the pain. It is whether or not we believe the pain is worth it, which reminds me of another thing from the 80s: At one point, I was a wrestler.

I wrestled from seventh grade through my sophomore year of high school. Four years of wrestling but not really, because, unlike football or basketball, I didn't wrestle at all out of season. So it was really around three months a year for four years. The total time was about twelve months of my life. It seems like it was a lot longer, though. It was absolute hell.

I apologize to all those out there who enjoy wrestling. I don't mean to say that wrestling is a terrible sport or without redeeming value. There were parts of it that I thoroughly enjoyed, but balancing those enjoyable parts with the hellish torment that was the majority of the season takes me even further down the rabbit trail and reminds me of hiking with my wife (Ouch. Sorry, honey).

I grew up in the Pacific Northwest, and up here, there are places where you can walk through a trail in a mountain forest, and it opens up upon a clearing with a mountain lake wrung by snow capped peaks. The water is crystal clear and smooth as glass. There are little patches of snow left over in areas where the sun never directly shines. It's beautiful. It inspires awe, and it brings people back to the mountains in this part of the world over and over again.

I have always enjoyed the mountains and especially enjoy vigorous activities in them, like hiking and skiing, so when I started dating my wife, I endeavored to include her in these loves. A year or so into our marriage, I had already tried and failed miserably to instill in her a love of skiing. With skiing off the table, I mistakenly concluded that hiking was the avenue that could finally get her hooked into an outdoor lifestyle.

Unfortunately, after a few attempts to slowly intro-duce Kari to the wonders of the PNW with day hikes and short excursions rather than producing a love of the great outdoors, I had only produced blisters and succeeded to introduce her to the existence of mole-skin and the need for better boots. After considerable deliberation, I decided that the destination of the hike was the true payoff and that by limiting her experience to day hikes, she wasn't able to fully enjoy the fruits of her labor by spending extended time in God's majestic creation in the Cascade Mountains.

I talked to my dad, and he consulted a friend of his who recommended a can't-miss, four-hour hike over mostly level ground culminating at a serene mountain lake with ample space to pitch tents and enjoy the scenery. From that idyllic location, after sleeping in the mountain air and enjoying a surprisingly good breakfast (I swear, my mom could pull a well-cooked meal out of her back pocket), we chose to tack on a day hike up to another mountain lake that would forever leave you dismissing every Bob Ross painting as chaotic scribbles on canvas.

This was my last shot. It was the bottom of the ninth, bases loaded, two outs, full count, and down by three. Kari and I had taken a few hikes. She had a good back-pack. She had her subpar footwear. She had seen some beauty, but it wasn't taking. She just wasn't enjoying it, and I was running out of pitches to hit the proverbial hiking homerun.

Years later, I now understand the uphill battle I had faced. My wife did not grow up in the woods. She was born in Lansing, Michigan, and grew up swimming competitively. There are a lot of things that competitive swimmers have in common, but one of those is that they grow up in extremely clean environments. They are literally always rinsing and washing. They sweat and work as hard or harder than most any other athlete, but much of their lives are spent submerged in chlorinated water. They don't feel the grime.

So, my Michigan girl felt—correction—feels no affinity toward the great outdoors, not if it involves sweat, dirt, and bugs, which, of course, it always does. So, this hike was meant to show her that here in the PNW, the beauty is so spectacular, and the destinations are so accessible, that a little strolling through the woods is totally worth it. There is gain after the pain!

I can still hear the sound of the wind as my bat sliced through the air connecting with nothing: swing and a miss. Strike three. You're out!

My parents, my brother and his wife, and Kari and I all took off for the trip together. Packed to the brim with food and luxuries to make this the most clean, bug-free, comfortable, and beautiful (and to be honest, romantic, because I'm a guy, and I live in perpetual hope that all experiences are interpreted as romantic) excursion my girl ever thought possible. My pack was about sixty pounds. My brother's and dad's were around seventy.

It was a lot of weight to carry, but most of it was food and liquids, and it was supposed to be a short hike. We would be much lighter when we returned, and it was worth it to set up the experience for Kari that I was shooting for. If done well, it was much more likely to be considered romantic. Right? (Don't laugh.)

So, we got started promptly about an hour later than we planned, drove up into the mountains, veered off onto a logging road, and followed it up to the trail head. The lateness of the start shouldn't have mattered since there was plenty of time for a three to four-hour hike, and there would still be enough time to enjoy camp before dark. However, the trail head was not clearly marked, so we took what seemed the most reasonable trail and headed out... for about thirty minutes until we were sure this reasonable trail was not the correct trail. Doubling back, we found the right one and started anew our hike to paradise.

It was now around 1 pm. The summer heat was getting to me a bit as I had already hiked for an hour with my pack, only to find myself back at the car. Also, we were now hiking in the heat of the day and heading out two hours later than we planned, but it was midsummer, and it didn't get dark in the PNW till around 9 pm. Three to four hours from then, I'd be soaking my feet in a mountain lake, and Kari would be won over with the beauty and accessibility of the mountains. It would all be worth it.

Instead, three hours later, Kari let me know that this was definitely not worth it. Her feet hurt, her pack was heavy, her water was gone, and, according to my dad, we still weren't 100 percent sure we were on the right trail. According to his friend, who informed us of this little gem, we should have come to a slight incline about an hour before, the top of which would have marked the finishing stretch to the lake. Yet, so far, we had simply hiked along a trail that gained altitude in the way you couldn't see with your eyes but felt in your legs.

As we passed through a fairly nondescript mountain meadow, I had a hard time spinning this experience in my head so I could continue to encourage my wife. My feet also hurt and my pack was also heavy, but by that time in my life, I had learned not to confront my wife's pain with expressions of my own. Little known to most hikers, the most dangerous animal in a forest is a wife with belittled pain.

We hiked on, and about thirty minutes later, my dad stopped at the beginning of an incline. Though to call it an incline is kind of like calling a motorcycle a bike. The name takes something daunting, and powerful and overemphasizes the fun and recreational aspects to diminish the danger. (Incline, my ass. This lake had better be beautiful!)

My wife took a chance to rest, and I casually walked up to my father and inspected the "trail" that essentially went straight up a hill and into the trees without end. It could have been a half-mile or three miles. There was no way to tell in the forest.

I looked back at my wife and knew this would be a disaster. This was a climb, not a hike. This would be a root-and-sapling grabbing, foothold finding, dirt-clawing scramble of an ascension for which I knew Kari was not prepared. She could do it, but being able to do something and being prepared to do something are light-years apart. What's worse was that prodding her up that hill would likely destroy my hopes for a romantic evening later.

Beyond that, we had no confidence in the time estimates anymore. We were 3.5 hours into a three to four-hour hike and had just reached what should have been a little over halfway. Did that mean we were an hour or so away from the lake or 3.5 hours away from the lake? And because of our late start and trail mishap, it was now 4:30, and the long end of the estimate could have us hiking in the dark on a poorly marked trail in the Cascade Mountains. No deal. It was time for damage control.

"Hey, honey. You know what we were thinking? That meadow back there was so beautiful and such a great place for a campsite. I think we are going to camp there for the night. It's been a long day, and we think it would be more enjoyable to spend time together around camp rather than push onward and not have together time. Ok?"

So we headed back. We pitched the tents and set up the cook stove. My mom knocked dinner out of the park. I can't remember what it was, I think seafood fettuccine, but I do remember wondering, not for the first time, how she did stuff like that. Resting our feet and laughing in a mountain meadow, my hope came back. My wife was smiling. I even caught a few fond looks my way that had been absent since about the forty-five-minute mark of that day's excursion. Maybe this wasn't a home run of a hike, but I was pretty sure I was stretching out a double.

We cleaned up, repacked what we could, hung up the food stuff in a tree, and headed to the tents for the kind of sleep you could only get in the mountains after a hike. And because I'm a guy, and I clearly can't read the room, I thought maybe there was a chance for a little more exercise.

"What are you doing?"

So, no more exercise. "I just thought..."

"No." Pause. I think, at this moment, she may have been processing the conflict between disbelief that her young husband was so clueless, disgust that he couldn't think of anything else, and a tiny bit of flattery that this stupid, shaggy dog of a man wanted her despite the sweat, grime, and fatigue.

She tried to explain what should have been readily obvious to any human with a fully functioning frontal lobe: "I'm tired, stinky, dirty, and your parents are ten feet away!"

That made me think, *Absolutely! That is so hot! You are so hot!* But what I said was, "You're not stinky. You're sexy," which I fully expected to work. I now think it triggered another response related to the first: the realization that her husband was not "like" a shaggy dog; he was literally a shaggy dog and must be dealt with as such. So, she gave me a firm, "No." At least she didn't hit me with a rolled up newspaper.

I rolled over and knew that sleep would find me very quickly, but before I could doze off, Kari very innocently said, "Why did you hang the food in the tree?"

Unthinkingly, I replied honestly, "So the bears don't get it."

"There are bears out here?!"

That is so cute.

Wait a second. If I played my manly protector cards right, maybe there was still a chance. "Of course there are bears. We are in the mountains. But don't worry. You're safe. I won't let anything happen to you."

"What are you going to do to stop a bear?!"

And then I knew I was toast. So, I pivoted and explained that they stayed away if there was no reason to come into the campsite. Bears didn't like people. They only looked for food left out, and we hung the food from a tree outside of our camp. We were safe. And I put my arm around her for comfort...

"I said, No!"

I rolled over and went to sleep.

I woke up the next morning completely refreshed. The crisp mountain air, birdsong, and the indirect sunlight of early morning produced a readiness for the day that I did not have at any other time in my life. I rolled over and said good morning to Kari because there was always a chance, right? But what stared back at me was not the refreshed, reinvigorated, slightly frisky woman that I hoped for. Instead, Kari looked back at me with fully awake but flat eyes ringed with the dark circles of too little sleep.

One other thing about my dad: he literally snores like a bear. I never really thought about it before that morning, but in the unique context of camping in the mountains, that description can be seen as more terrifying than humorous. As such, Kari had spent the night trapped in our little nylon bubble with thoughts of a hungry, man-eating bear traipsing through our campsite while hearing the rumble and snort of my father's sleep. The tension between knowing that the noise was coming from my dad, the fear of unzipping the tent to look, and the risk of waking me and possibly alerting some wild creature with only a millimeter of woven plastic as protection kept her huddled and wide-eyed in her sleeping bag for much of the night. It was not the fresh re-start I was hoping for (strike three. You're out).

The rest of the trip was fairly uneventful. After breakfast and roughly thirty minutes of a steep climb, it turned out that the lake was only a little over an hour away from our campsite. It really was beautiful. We spent the rest of the day relaxing and enjoying the water and the scenery, and the following morning, we hiked back to the car, concluding the last hike my wife ever went on.

Talking to her later, she admitted that it was beautiful. It just wasn't worth it. The dirt, bugs, bears, and blisters were not erased by the scenery and cool waters of the mountain lake, which was the reason I started this story with wrestling; while the discomfort of hiking was worth it for me to get to the lake or see the scenery, it was not worth it for my wife, and that is exactly how I felt about wrestling.

I was a good wrestler, but it was by far the hardest thing I have ever done. And before you dismiss my Western-civilized, middle-class softness, keep in mind that I have already explained the relative nature of pain, and it is an undeniably painful sport. Wrestling was like doing the Bataan Death March every day! Childbirth has nothing on wrestling! Stubbing my toe?! Pshaw! Ok, that is a massive exaggeration, but it is really, really hard.

Sucking weight, long, arduous workouts, cardiovascular exercise, strength training; wrestling forced me to complete the hardest workouts I have ever endured. Hikes from hell, football two-a-days, and basketball lines, CrossFit... not even close. Wrestling eclipses them all, probably because it is immensely difficult from both a physical and psychological aspect.

The bottom line for me is that in all the years I wrestled and during the many times I have watched it (much more enjoyable to watch), the vast majority of matches were lost due to physical exhaustion or psychological defeat rather than anything else. Skill plays a part, for sure, but foremost, wrestling is a sport dictated by toughness. You must endure and overcome. If you don't, you are in danger of being rolled onto your back in the middle of a gymnasium in front of dozens of witnesses. There is no middle ground in wrestling. There is no hiding. When a wrestler loses, there is almost always an element of shame that he deals with because, at some point, he knows that inside, he said, "I quit."

I was pretty good at it. From a skill point of view, I was average, but one thing I have always been good at is persevering. I don't quit. I hate quitting, and that quality served me well in wrestling. When I lost, it was almost always because I ran up against someone by whom I was simply outclassed. But at the junior high and high school level, that didn't happen often. Mostly, I just out-toughed my opponents. I outlasted them. I could handle the defeats mainly because they didn't come very often, and since I won a fair amount, I got to enjoy the flip-side of lying prone in the middle of a gymnasium—the unique pride that comes from physically and mentally conquering someone in public.

I really liked what wrestling did to my body too. I was strong, lean, and pretty confident that I could take just about anyone that came my way. But these perks don't just fall out of the sky.

To get better, you have to wrestle those who are better; you have to beat your body[1] into submission, so while I won my share of matches, I consistently lost during practice. I worked out harder than I ever had in my life, and I reduced my weight as much as I could. The result was that I dreaded practice. Exhaustion and defeat were everyday experiences, but I knew they would pay off in the long run. Mostly, I absolutely hated sucking weight. Combining the hardest exercise I had ever experienced with daily repetition and reduced calories was beyond difficult. To do it through Thanksgiving, Christmas, college football bowl season, and New Years—torture. Ultimately, for me, and like my wife with hiking, it just wasn't worth it.

So, for the first time in my life, at the end of my sophomore season, I quit. I never went back. I could not justify the pain of the sport, both physical and psychological, with the payoff. Just like it is for all of us, my willingness to endure pain is completely dependent on the value I place on the outcome of that pain.

This is at the heart of the second lie. Pain is not bad, but pain without gain has no redeeming value. Nobody wants to experience pain for no reason. That probably isn't a point we need to discuss at length, but because conversations about pain almost always center around tragedy and torture, seemingly valueless instances of pain, we often contemplate pain without contemplating the outcome. Pain is painted with the broad brush of negativity and sometimes even evil. This just isn't accurate.

I have vivid memories of lining up for rounds of sprints during football practices in August. I know this experience isn't at the height of pain you can experience in this world or even near the top of the pain I have experienced in my life, but at the moment, it was excruciating. I didn't believe I had any more to give. I was exhausted. I just wanted to lay down on the 110-degree astro-turf and melt. But the coach would yell out, "Again!" So, I'd drag my butt back to the line and get in my stance while my pads, which had been loosened by heat and sweat, seemed to twist around my chest and legs. The sweat was in my eyes and mouth. I had one hand on the ground and did my best to keep my back level and knees bent. My legs didn't even burn anymore. They were just numb.

The coach would yell, "On two!" and would do his best to get us to start at the wrong time. Some moron would always jump offsides (sometimes that moron was me), and we would move backward five yards and start again. And again. And again. I hated those moments.

The weird thing is that I don't remember those times with any kind of negative emotion. Looking back, there is pride in the memory, even a little humor. The pain I experienced on those August days do not sit in my brain in the same bucket as taking a softball off my shin at third base, flying over the handlebars of my bicycle and splitting my lip and nose on the pavement, or being rejected at the ninth-grade dance. There is no "pain bucket." The filter is my perception of the outcome, not the pain itself.

I have no doubt that other people on the football field with me during those days do not remember sprints the way I do. I am certain that some of my teammates cringe at the description of being yelled at and manipulated into running "Again!" But I loved football. It was worth it. It was a hike in the woods, and the games were mountain lakes. For me, there was gain from the pain.

The truth is that pain is ultimately neither a bad thing nor a good thing. It is just a tool, and the use of that tool is what we interpret as valuable or not.

Pain keeps us safe. Without pain, there are no safety rails in our lives. It is immensely difficult to learn without the existence of pain. The fear of failure, feeling of loss, consequence of not passing or graduating, and never wanting to be burned again—these things drive us to remember. They cement knowledge, behavioral changes, and thought processes in our heads.

I think we know this on an instinctual level. Maybe this is why we seek out painful experiences that we expect to produce positive results. We hope to cement that learning or accomplishment through struggle. I will push to exercise harder in expectation that the fitness sticks and builds upon itself. I will endure the stress of asking for a promotion in hopes of attaining a permanent step forward. I will nervously approach the girl to achieve the relationship. I will fight the fight to put it to an end, once and for all. I will even inflict pain on others in expectation that they learn: spanking, prison, running sprints, detention, or the silent treatment. And while we all understand that these tactics are not always effective—pain does not guarantee learning or growth—we also understand that learning or growth doesn't take place without pain. Easy things never stick.

But it has to be worth it. I have to value the outcome. It has to be worth it to me, not just some general good thing, something of value.[2]

Count it all joy...[3]

Chapter 4

C'mon. Just Tell Me.

I REMEMBER THE 2004 presidential election pretty clearly. I was a few years into a profession in the financial industry, and the economy had mostly recovered after the dot-com bubble popping, followed by the double whammy of 9/11. George W. Bush was running for reelection. The Federal Reserve was steadily raising rates after it had dropped to an all-time low of 1 percent in June of 2003. Real estate was on the rise with historically low mortgage rates now below 6 percent. Unemployment rates had steadily decreased for that past year, but after a strong stock market climb through 2003, the markets were largely flat to negative heading into the election. As a relative newbie to the financial world, I was perplexed. Sure, there were questions and risks, but there were always questions and risks surrounding the markets. It just didn't seem like it made any sense. With all this good news and positive momentum, why was the stock market flat?

That was the first time I heard the adage "markets hate uncertainty." At the time, it seemed way too glib of an explanation to the complex movements of the capital markets, but without going into all the intricacies of economic principles and the forward-looking nature of Wall Street, this adage, accurately, if not comprehensively, explains much of the macro movements in America's investment industry. And barring significant events like the crash of 2008 and the lockdowns of 2020, presidential election years always seem to boil down to this fact: Wall Street is largely ambivalent to whether Democrats or Republicans win the White House; they just want to know who it will be. Or, said more simply: Investors just want to be relatively confident of the outcome so they can plan accordingly. Or, said more globally: When the outlook is uncertain, people avoid risk until they are more confident in the outcome.

If that sounds mundane, too simple, or, like me, too glib of an explanation of how the largest economy in the history of the world operates, allow me to let you in on a secret that almost everyone learns in the financial industry: It is run by people. The market isn't money, companies, or computers. The economy isn't charts, graphs, or numbers. It is people; people shopping, saving, investing, performing jobs, losing their houses, borrowing money, or any number of things. It is all people.

Regardless of whether you are Jamie Dimon, Warren Buffet, or John Q. Public, you are still a person with the same fears, choices, and dynamics that affect us all. We are all evaluating risk, reward, pain, and outcomes. We are all trying to figure out if the hike is worth it. The scale may change, but the calculation is the same; if the perceived outcome is greater than the pain, then ok.

This truth isn't limited to Wall Street. It is true all the way up to the heights of power structures. One of the most remarkable shifts in human history was the creation of the United States of America. And before you dismiss that claim as jingoistic, pro-American tripe, consider that with all of its flaws, the Declaration of Independence sparked the pivot in world history from an almost universally monarchial and theocratic governance in virtually every corner of the world to today's proliferation of democratic principles almost equally as broad. The secession of the American colonies from Great Britain broke the link from the European monarchial system and the church as a governing body, and the foundational reason behind it was an understanding that regardless of power or position or progeny or professed faith, people are people. On the inside, kings and presidents (and CEOs, pastors, and police officers) are the same insecure, self-protecting, self-promoting beings that we all are. And our founders knew that it was folly to assume that a king, senator, or mayor would consistently act in the best interest of others. Their power was granted and had to be limited.

Like the kings and queens of old and titans of American commerce today, we all want pleasure, prosperity, growth, and power of some degree, and we are all willing to sacrifice for whatever it is we want, but first, we put the risk and the reward through the pain calculation.

It is a value proposition. I want the candy bar. I'm willing to sacrifice one dollar for the candy bar. I am not willing to sacrifice two dollars for the candy bar. The value of two dollars (or said differently, the pain losing two dollars) is greater than the outcome of the candy bar, so I won't do it—economics. So, in very broad terms (and recognizing there are unmentioned complexities worthy of discussion), our daily lives boil down to risk reward decisions. What will I get? What will I lose?

Personality plays a role here as well. Not all people will approach this calculation in the same way. Some start with the reward: That looks fun. That money could be mine. They will all love me. I'm going to win the game. It is key to understand that "reward" is not a clearly defined thing. Reward is defined by individual and cultural definitions of value. While there are many similarities between people on what is valued—life, wealth, love, security, fame, power—the hierarchy or prioritization of values is internal and very individual.

Within the same culture, different individuals may value wealth, but it may fall in significantly different places in a list of priorities. For one, it may be the top value in his life while another may value life experiences above material possessions. And these values shift over time. At one point in my life, the desire for a lover may be my highest goal, while later, security for myself and for the wife I have found shifts to the top. The point being is that we all seek reward, but there are vast differences in what each individual will sacrifice in order to attain similar benefits, because, like in the candy bar example, risk and reward and value and cost are inextricably linked.

While many people start with the identification of the goal or reward, many others (in fact, I think most people) begin the calculation by identifying the risk or cost: danger, pain, loss, rejection, shame, embarrassment, FOMO, FOBO... As I mentioned, some of us go through life recognizing the potential rewards and opportunities available, and then, sometimes as an afterthought, we do a risk calculation to temper our ambition, greed, or desire. But many, if not most of us, do the exact opposite. We primarily navigate life by identifying risks, avoiding them, and waiting for the reward to push us out of our fear and into action. The job, relationship, experience, or position is almost a second thought. I reflect on it. I determine that she is worth the risk and there is a probability I am comfortable with that I will achieve the goal. I'm still afraid, but I work up the courage. Then I act.

This is a very different order from the first person. For the reward first person, it may look more like I want that. I'm going after it. Wait a second. This looks like it may be blowing up. Damage control. Pivot. Regardless of order, it is essentially the same calculation. How much do I want it? How much pain am I willing to endure to get it?

This is all very interesting and, for most of us, fairly intuitive, but when we climb down from the ivory tower of theoretical discussions and enter the real world, there is one factor that throws the whole pain calculation into a tail spin: We can't see the future. This is why "the market hates uncertainty." If Wall Street, and by Wall Street, I mean the people who make up the investing industry, can't predict within an acceptable range of probability, they simply won't invest.

Understand that there are varying degrees of this. Sometimes we are more sure of an outcome than others. Sometimes we only perceive one acceptable choice. But many times in our lives, we come to a crossroads, look down each path, and see nothing but ambiguity. Regardless of whether, in that moment, I am leading with risk or reward; the problem is that I cannot see the actual future reward or risk.

The woman I love may not stay the same. She may not continue to love me. I may not continue to love her.

The job I want may turn out to be more tedious and frustrating than the one I have now. There may be pain, or there may not be pain. If I ask for a promotion, start my own business, or ask her out, the answer may be yes and, had I known that, the decision would have been easy. It turns out the pain I was worried about didn't exist. If I had known *that*, I never would have hesitated.

If only I could know the outcome in those situations. Or even if I could know a little bit of the outcome, it would be so much less stressful. And that brings me back one more time to "markets hate uncertainty," which is kind of a stupid saying because it makes it sound like this is something unique to "markets," when the truth is "people hate uncertainty."[4]

I met Kari in fifth grade. It was not love at first sight. Well, maybe it was... kind of. She was new to my school as a fourth grader, a year behind me. She had this short, lopsided, asymmetrical haircut that I found pretty cute (I would say attractive, but my fifth-grade self thought she was "cute"). It showed off her neck and jawline. My wife has a great jaw. Not sure why I like that so much, but I am a sucker for a jawline.

I saw her across the soccer field and thought, "Huh! Who is that!?" So, as many fifth graders are apt to do, I meandered in that direction; not that I was going to talk to her. Lord, no! Of course not. I just wanted to get a better look. This young lioness had wandered into my territory, and I needed to investigate.

I was like the leader of the pride stalking a potential queen. I picked out my path, one that was upwind so I didn't spook her; one that seemed natural. As any hunter knows, she would see me long before I was close enough to get a good look at her. It was a safe path, one that would approach her vicinity without risking actual interaction, one that looked coincidental, not intentional; one that said, "I'm not a threat. You don't have to kill me." But still, it was one that brought me close enough that I could get a better look at the lopsided-hair goddess of cuteness that had descended upon Mukilteo Elementary.

I wandered over in the direction of the tetherball poles. I acted like I was interested in this one game that no one in the school played. I peeked out of the corner of my eye to make sure she was still congregating with the other lionesses. She was still there, maybe a bit further away than I thought, but still there. I moved on toward 4-Square, shooed the third-grade meerkats out of the way, and checked again. Dang it! I didn't seem to draw as close as I had planned. It's as if she was drifting slightly away from me whenever I broke eye contact.

It was time for a change of plans. I looked toward her but off to the side as if I saw something in the distance. Young boys are keenly aware that fourth-grade girls have the eyesight of a peregrine falcons. I may not have been able to see her well, but I knew she could tell where I was looking, so I kept my eyes off center and began to walk toward my fictitious destination. My route should take me within ten feet of my prey, but if I didn't slow down or make any jerky movements, she likely wouldn't pounce. I was sweating. This was a much more dangerous tact than I was usually comfortable with, but at that point, survival had become a secondary concern. The hunt had become my entire focus.

As I approached her, though, the world began to slow its rotation. The fuzzy peripheral image of my eventual mate grew too rapidly. She was closer than I had planned! The scale was off! She wasn't a normal girl. She was huge!

Like any experienced hunter, I turned. I didn't run. I simply jogged away like I had just remembered something I had left in Indiana.

It turned out that Kari grew early. She was over five feet tall in fourth grade, which, at the time, projected to be likely ten-foot six by adulthood, and I wasn't going to approach her unless I at least had a sling and five smooth stones.

Of course, my projection of her eventual height was not accurate. Eventually, Kari topped out at five-foot four, and I passed her up. I grew into my eventual, below-average height, and as she plateaued into mortal proportions, my attraction for her grew again, but that took years. In the meantime, I developed a different conclusion about dating than most of my friends.

I was a relatively popular kid. I was smart and funny. I was a good athlete. I was not really the best at anything, but good at most everything, so I didn't struggle in the ways that many do through middle school. I kept things light and positive on the outside. Inside, though, I was also a pretty serious kid. I felt deeply but kept it under wraps. My friends wouldn't have been aware of the emotions rolling below the surface, except maybe anger, which seemed less risky to let out at times.

With strong flows of emotions mixed with twelve to fourteen-year-old hormones, I fell for girls hard. I didn't let them know it, of course. I played the game, flirted, joked, and pretended I was much more confident than I really was. But the indirectness of communication, manipulation, and short-term nature of middle school relationships played havoc with my heart.

Casual relationships simply weren't interesting to me. Even though I wasn't ready for it, and it seemed like I was alone in the pursuit, I was actively looking for love. It wasn't anyone else's fault that they weren't. We were in middle school. Most kids are just trying to navigate fourth period, not find their soul mate.

By the end of ninth grade, I couldn't take it anymore. I remember the exact moment that the scale tipped for me. I left the ninth-grade dance and went outside by myself. Nothing had gone wrong. If I was even remotely normal, this should have been a really good night. I had just enjoyed being the center of attention, dancing and joking. I looked around and saw a few girls that clearly liked me. I saw a couple more that didn't. I saw one I liked a lot but always seemed to give me mixed signals: nice to me in person, stand-offish in groups. Of course, now I know how normal this was, but for a sensitive and serious kid, I didn't understand it at the time.

Anyway, something just broke. The song ended. I said I was hot, and I walked outside by myself. I sat down and started crying. I don't really know why. I had all of this emotion pent up inside me. I was tired. I couldn't see how joking, preening, and showing off would to lead to anything more than wondering what the girl in the group across the gym thought about me.

The crying didn't last long, just a minute or so. Really, I was just immature, confused, and hadn't learned yet that to have a relationship, you have to cross the gym and take a risk. But on that night, regardless of my perspective now, the pain was real. It was a ten, and I had reached a tipping point. So I prayed.[5] I told God that I wanted a wife. I told him that I was clearly bad at picking one out and said that I knew he knew me better than I knew myself,[6] and he knew my future wife better than I ever could, so I would just wait for him to let me know. And I told him I had only one condition. I told him that I was pretty dense, and I needed her to be direct—no more hints and guesses. I wasn't going to play the games anymore. When he had someone for me, he should just let me know. Right there, in the courtyard outside the ninth-grade dance, I laid it all out for God and left it in his hands. As nuts as that sounds, I really meant it, and I followed through with it.

From that point forward, I stopped hanging out with girls. I didn't avoid them. I still noticed them. I still wanted them. It was just that interactions were now more incidental rather than intentional. I had friends that were girls. I had some girls that were interested in me. I just didn't engage. I went to dances. I went on a couple of dates. But I never went on more than one because I was waiting for God to let me know. In my mind, I had been very clear. I had told him what I needed and how he was to get my attention, and I trusted him to follow through.

A couple of years later, Kari showed up again, this time in my chemistry class, and yes, she was still cute. She was funny, outgoing, and smart (and not six-foot ten). Unfortunately, her hair was now symmetrical, but I could look past that. I flirted and even went to a soccer game with her once, but true to form, despite my attraction, I didn't let the relationship progress any further.

Almost a year later, we ended up at a before-the-school-year-school leadership retreat together. There was laughing, talking, and more flirting. My resolve was failing, but not in an undisciplined way. It was more of a "she is kind of what I've been looking for—do you think..." kind of way. But right after the retreat, the teachers in our district went on strike, and we ended up starting school a month late. In the meantime, I was quickly distracted from the feelings that had begun to develop at the retreat. I was playing football. I was the ASB president. It was my senior year, and, believe it or not, I was pretty self-absorbed.

Because of the strike, when we started school again, it was already October. We had to rush to put on homecoming, and since Kari and I were both in student leadership, we ended up seeing each other again that week. True to form, I was taking a friend of mine to the dance because that is what I did. There was no reason to break the pattern. God hadn't told me yet.

That week became one of the most memorable times of my life, but despite what teen movies would have you believe, neither the football game, nor the homecoming ceremony, nor the homecoming dance hold any permanent spot in my memory. They just weren't important. There are three things that I do remember very clearly, though.

First, on Wednesday before the big homecoming court assembly where the king and queen were announced (spoiler—it wasn't me), Kari and I headed over to McDonald's to grab some lunch beforehand. I don't really know how we ended up doing this together. It wasn't really a date. Sure, we had flirted a bit over the years, and she wasn't nearly as scary anymore, but as far as I knew, we were friends. I don't remember what we ate. I don't remember what we talked about. However,

I do remember her hair, what she wore, and how she looked at me because she said, "Why didn't you ask me to the dance?"

That simple question rocked my world. This wasn't in the girl playbook that I was familiar with. This was direct. This was straight to the point. So, I replied honestly, "I didn't know you wanted me to," which was absolutely true. Probably the only reason I hadn't asked her to homecoming was that I didn't know she wanted me to. (Contrary, again, to most teen movies, I believe what drives most males to ask someone out is perceived knowledge of attraction. *If you like me, then I'm interested.* The risk is mediated, so full speed ahead.)

Even though she had already laid down three aces of directness, and I was reeling, trying to process how my worldview of indirect human interaction had just shifted below my feet, she followed up with a pair of kings—the full house of relational beginnings. "Well, I did. I like you and wanted you to ask me to the dance."

Mind blown!

Angels singing.

Faith confirmed.

Thank you, God.

Wife met.

I have no idea what else was said that day and no clue about the assembly, the game, or the dance. I have no idea about much of anything. I think I was thoroughly in my own head because while this isn't a great story, that conversation spoke right to my heart. I can't explain it completely, but as I sat across from Kari with her teased 1990 hair and god-awful blue, white, and black outfit (still don't know what to call it—kind of shorts with matching top, but kind of like an 80s power suit that was tailored for an English school boy—it was a weird time for fashion), her words fulfilled exactly what I had prayed for back in ninth grade.

I knew it was crazy. My rational mind kept saying that I was eighteen (almost), that you don't decide who you are going to marry based on three sentences said over a Big Mac, that high school romances don't last, that your first real girlfriend (which she wasn't... yet) doesn't turn out to be who you spend your life with. But I couldn't shake the feeling. I couldn't reconcile my mind with my heart.

We won the football game. I was told that I played the best game of my life. I don't remember any of it; not a clue. Maybe I had a concussion. But, of course, while I can't remember playing the game, the second thing I remember from that week, clear as crystal, was the moments immediately following the game.

The spectators all came out onto the field. I was talking to my parents. It was a tradition for us to go out and grab a slice of pie after my football games. I love pie. It is absolutely my favorite thing. And, I loved talking with my parents about the game. My dad was a football coach and could always give me real talk about the game, my play, the key points. My mom was a mom. So, I was awesome, and who doesn't want to hear that? While I talked to them, probably beginning the recap of my awesomeness, Kari came run-skipping across the field. This was something she did—run-skip: arms straight down to her side and run a few steps, skip, hop, skip, run a few steps again... She ran-skipped right up to me, hugged me, and told me something like congratulations or something. Actually, I have no idea what she said or how long she talked, because she had just hugged me and that was the best thing ever! The only thing that registered besides the hug was that she and some friends were heading over to Denny's and "Would you like to come?" For the first time in my life, I didn't want to grab some pie with my parents. Friday night chain diner food sounded like a much better choice.

The next morning, I went to football practice. This was something our coach always did. He said it had to do with staying on top of injuries, which I know was part of it. He didn't want us sitting on sprained ankles all weekend and prolonging our time out of play. But we all knew that the real, underlying reason was prevention or punishment of after-game partying. It is not wise to party too hard on Friday night when you know you will be running wind sprints on Saturday morning.

The third thing I remember was after practice. I walked up to the school and found Kari setting up for the dance. I hung out, helped, talked, drove her home, got pulled over by the police, met her parents, watched some hockey (for the second time in my life), and went home. I can still picture what the dance set up looked like. I can picture her in the car with me. I can describe the police officer who pulled me over. I can picture her parents watching the game, the big screen TV, and the lighting in the room. I don't remember the rest of the day or the dance that night. I don't remember anything other than calling Kari after I dropped my date off and talking on the phone with her while her date was in the other room.

I won't say I was in love. Being "in love" sounds like a condition, like a sprained ankle or a headache. Being "in love" sounds like being "in pain," current and temporary. I wasn't "in love." I loved her. In three days, she had checked all my boxes. She was beautiful, funny, intelligent, confident, and direct. She told me what she thought and wanted. And I knew then, weeks before my eighteenth birthday, I wanted to marry her. I knew it was improbable at best, but I knew.

Thirty years later, we've been married for over twenty-five years. I won't say it has always been smooth. For the most part, I have been a good husband, but I have also been selfish and thoughtless. I have lied and broken trust. I have said and done mean things, but I have always been committed to her because Kari will always be God's gift to me. God looked down into my fifteen-year-old brokenness, and two and a half years later, presented me with the answer to my prayer. He saw me alone, in pain, and gave me someone to go through it with me.

To walk away from that would be to say that I don't need what God knows I do. It would be to deny my own knowledge of myself, and it would be to take something similar from my wife.

Only if the rest of life were so clear. I can't tell you how many times I have repeated some form of that ninth-grade prayer. "God, just tell me. Just make it clear. Open the door. Close the door. Show me what you would have me do. C'mon, God. Just tell me!" But God almost never answers this prayer the way he did with my wife.

After experiencing such a clear answer to prayer that met me in my fear and disappointment, the lack of repeated success caused ongoing questioning and angst over the next ten odd years. I couldn't understand why God didn't consistently give me the clarity and foresight that I was looking for. "C'mon, God! Just tell me!"

This was precisely what I had prayed for as a teenager—clarity. I just wanted to meet a woman who told me clearly who she was, what she wanted, and what she thought. "You gave that to me. Why won't you give me clarity in other things?"

"Am I supposed to be a teacher? I want to be obedient. I want to follow your will in my life. If you are calling me to be a teacher, let me know."—Nothing.

"Is this the right time to have children? Kari and I are both still very young. We are both teachers and don't make a lot of money. I want to do what is in your will."—Nada.

"Should I pursue this degree in counseling? I love working with kids. I love helping, coaching, and guiding them. This is a huge expense. Is this where you would have me go? Is this what you want me to do?"—Zip.

"Should I stick with what I'm doing or move for a new job? I would be taking a huge risk. I have a new child and a rocky marriage. There is no guarantee of success. I'd be putting all my eggs in this basket and risking my family and stability. God, at least close the door if I'm not supposed to do it."—Nothing. "Does that mean the door is still open, or are you just leaving me hanging again?"

It was after asking this last question that I finally heard God's answer, and it wasn't because it was the first time that he spoke. It was really because it was the first time that I listened. I was filtering. I don't think I am alone in this. We listen for the answer we want or the answer we are expecting rather than listening to the person in a conversation by actively and attentively paying attention to what is said and, more importantly, what is meant. I think in many conversations and especially in prayer, what we do is closer to listening for our name in a crowded room. Everyone is talking, and it amounts to a bunch of noise, and then you hear your name. You are attuned to it and can filter out all the other noise to clearly hear that one thing you are always listening for, consciously or subconsciously. Before that last question, I was filtering. I was attuned to the one answer I was looking for. God was telling me something else entirely, but it was only noise in a crowded room.

That day, when I asked God about changing careers, I was a bit more desperate to hear from him. After so many perceived silences, I just wanted to hear something. And I did.

Don't misunderstand me here. I didn't hear an audible voice of God. There was no shaking of the earth or thunder from the heavens. God does not primarily speak that way. As in the story of Elijah, God was not in the earthquake. God was not in the wind. God was not in the fire. God was in the whisper.[7]

God speaks, but he doesn't demand our attention. Small, insecure people need to yell. They raise their voices because they are looking for validation from their audience. They need to be heard for the recognition of their wisdom, the affirmation of their place. God does not need my recognition, affirmation, or validation. He loves me, so he speaks to me. He loves me, so he allows me to go my own way. He loves me, so he speaks in a still, small voice, and if I choose to listen, his Word is there for the having.

God, should I move or not? Should I pursue this job or not? For the first time, I listened. I was quiet. I was sincere. And I heard him. "Go or don't go. Stay or don't stay. I am with you where you are. I will be with you if you stay or if you go."[8]

All of the pieces of my life shifted and began to fall into place. Scripture I had read or heard; prayers, answers, and non-answers; sermons, conversations, and thoughts—a thread began to materialize through them. Dots began to connect.

God is many things, but one of those things is a father, and as a father, he wants what is best for us, not what is easy for us. He wants me to grow into a man, not to remain a boy. He does not want me to experience pain, but he is willing to let me. He is willing to inflict pain as punishment. He is willing to allow pain as a consequence for my choices. He is willing to let me experience pain as a result of my being a man with my own choices and life. He will not keep me in a bubble. He will not protect me from all evil.

A few years ago, my wife heard Michelle Poler speak on her hundred-days-without-fear experiment. Michelle is a woman who undertook an exercise of confronting one hundred fears in one hundred days. Each day, she looked a fear directly in the face and pushed through it. It is a really cool story, but one thing she said, my wife repeated to me, and it has stuck ever since. She said, "The longer you stay in your comfort zone, the smaller it gets."

Just like the financial markets, I want clarity because I want to measure the risk before plunging into a decision. I want the comfort that comes along with a measured decision. But God the Father will not leave me in my comfort zone because that is not in my best interest.

It is not good for us to avoid all pain. The less pain in our lives, the more it cripples us. Pain is useful. It warns us from danger, and it is necessary for growth. Without it, we atrophy. But with good pain, comes bad.

Some pain is harmful. Sometimes it is malicious or without purpose. But God loves us, and just like any good father, he allows the pain but doesn't abandon us to it.

As my father, he lets me climb the tree in the backyard. It is something I want to do. It's fun and adventurous. I learn independence by doing it myself. I confront my fear and learn I can push through it. I develop muscles that allow me to pull and push my body to new heights. I develop confidence in doing something that seems daunting. I gain perspective from a new viewpoint.

And I fall.

And break my arm.

And my father is there to comfort me in my pain. He makes sure I get the treatment I need. He sits with me for weeks as I struggle through the itching from the cast. He talks to me when I am sad for missing out on playing baseball with my friends. And when I get the cast off, he pushes me to climb the tree again because my father knows that I would never climb the tree if I knew I was going to fall. He knows the risks involved in living life. And he knows the risks of sheltering his son from that risk. And God *always* chooses freedom and life. So, instead of giving us certainty, instead of eliminating pain, he gives us freedom. He knows that with freedom comes risk, and with risk comes pain. To eliminate pain is to eliminate freedom. He accepts it for our best interest but commits to being with us when it eventually comes.

And that is what I missed staring at the woman I love over a Big Mac on a Wednesday in October when Kari told me she liked me. I had prayed to God as a ninth grader that God would make it clear to me who my wife was. My motivation was to avoid heartbreak. I didn't want to go through the pain of looking for a wife. I didn't want to cross the gym. I didn't want to risk rejection. I didn't want to expose the serious kid that was hidden beneath my middle-school persona. I wanted the easy button. I wanted life without risk. So, during homecoming week of my senior year of high school, I thought God had answered my prayer of protecting me from pain.

This sounds ridiculous to me now. Has anyone ever avoided pain by getting married? Marriage is full of pain. Marriage results in pain! But the pain is worth it.

Over the years, Kari and I have fought and cried. We have seen counselors. We have struggled with betrayal, isolation, and mistrust. We have grieved. We have had crises of faith. We have looked at the bills and wondered what we would possibly do next. We have experienced petrifying fear.

And we have stayed with each other. And we have grown. And we have loved, laughed, cried, and hugged. We have felt the immense pride that only a parent can feel. We have wondered in awe at the creation of our four children. We have had excesses of money, love, and joy. We have experienced deliverance from addiction, fear, and depression. And I couldn't have made it without her.

Back in the fall of 1990, I was so focused on the answer I was listening for that I thought God gave it to me. But God didn't answer my ninth-grade prayer in the way I thought he had. He didn't give me the clarity to avoid risk. He didn't grant me a reprieve from pain. He granted me a partner *in* the pain.

Out of weakness, I asked for clarity, and he answered by giving me the strength to navigate the uncertainty. He gave someone to me that would, yes, cause me a great deal of pain in my life, but more importantly, a woman that would walk through it with me, that would be with me while my arm mended and would push me to climb the tree again. Because since the beginning, God knew, "It is not good for man to be alone."[9]

CHAPTER 5

HELP ME!

I WOULD NOT be the man I am today without my wife. That isn't just a platitude. Kari has been instrumental in my ability to cope and persevere through the many heartaches of the past thirty years. Without her, I simply wouldn't be as good of a man as I am today. I'm not saying that I'm a great man. I just wouldn't be this good without her. She has held me accountable. She has taught me to love better. She has forgiven me when I could not forgive myself. She has been a rock when I felt swept away by the stream.

I'm also not saying that I couldn't have survived on my own. I'm sure I would have made it through, some way or another. I can persevere. I'm tough enough. But I am certain that I would not have learned, matured, or grown as much as I have without her in my life.

The bottom line for me is that while I can survive on my own, survival is not necessarily a good thing. Life is good. Truly living is good. Existence... meh.

If you exist though, there is at least one certainty: You will experience pain. It is unavoidable. In this world, in this life, you will have trouble.[10] There is no escaping it. No one knows the form or severity of that pain, but we do know it exists, and its existence is useful. The question then is not how to eliminate pain from our lives but how to deal with it.

In Genesis 2:18, when God says, "It is not good for man to be alone...", I don't think it is just a passing phrase or literary transition. This is a fundamental truth about the nature of human beings. It is not good that we be alone.

Before breaking this out a bit more, I want to acknowledge the gravity of Genesis 2:18. Regardless of whether you are Christian, Jewish, Muslim, Hindu, Atheist, Buddhist, or whatever, the creation stories as described in the Bible get to the heart of humanity. Furthermore, the creation stories in Genesis are not exclusively Christian. These accounts predate Jesus Christ and the birth of Islam and Judaism. These accounts are shared by faiths, and even if you put your faith in a belief that there is no God, the truths that are expressed in these stories are worth noting.

If you are not familiar with these stories, the second account of creation, which begins at Genesis 2:4, is essentially a summary with insight into the particular episode of creating man and woman. In verses 4-17, God creates the world and the first man, Adam. He creates a garden in the midst of a land of abundant fertility and resources, and he places Adam in that garden. Regardless of how you view the accounts of creation in the book of Genesis, whether this is literal, figurative, poetic, or theological, the account of the creation of the world has significance. Why are we here? Why are things the way they are? What started this whole mess?

While Genesis does not offer exhaustive answers to these and other questions, it does offer glimpses. So before going on to verse 18, think about the situation described up to this point. Think about it in the context of the text.

Adam is in paradise. He is without sin. We can safely assume that no man in the Bible other than Jesus lived more closely with God than Adam did. This should be it then, right? There should be no more to the story. End the Bible here at Genesis 2:17.

No sin? Check.

Closeness with God? Check.

Paradise? Check.

Then, everything is good. Right?

Wrong.

Any close reading of verse 18 should cause you pause. In the first creation account in Genesis 1:1–2:3, God comments regularly on his creation. The light is good

(1:3). The seas and land are good (1:10). The plants are good (1:13). The sun, moon, and stars are good (1:18). The creatures of the air and sea are good (1:21). The creatures of the land are good (1:25). Man and woman and everything he made are all *very* good (1:31). But in the second account, in verse 2:18, in the midst of a seemingly perfect situation, God looks at Adam and says, "It is *not* good that the man should be alone…"

In the midst of producing a *very* good creation, God verbally acknowledges a potential defect in the product, a potential flaw in the design that cannot be ignored. While the trees, plants, sea, air, sky, and Adam are good, it is *not* good that he be alone.

This, by itself, is a perception altering statement. Again, regardless of your faith background, the creation story gets to the heart of our understanding of who we are as people, and in it God says that it is not good for us to be alone. But keep this in mind: Adam wasn't alone. He had the animals, and more importantly, he had God.

Adam may not have been alone in the garden in the sense of proximity. He was close to the animals and he was in the same space as God. He may not even have been alone spiritually. However, in terms of his navigation through his life, Adam was alone. He was alone in his efforts and pursuits. In verse 20, it says there was no suitable helper for Adam, and this is what was not good. So, God rectifies the situation by creating Eve.

Now, there is a danger in overanalyzing this passage.[11] It is important not to infer what is not said in this passage. This passage does not comment on the nature of God's relationship with us. It does not comment on the roles of men and women in society. It does not exhaustively address relationships in any way. And it does not speak to many, many other things either.

It does make some things very clear, though. A fundamental truth of life from the very beginning of humanity is that it is not good to go through the endeavor of life alone. Proximity is not the same thing as community. It is not the same to be near someone as to have a helper or, said differently, a roommate is not necessarily a teammate. And perhaps most shockingly, God implies that a relationship with God alone is not sufficient for our lives here on earth. He is the bedrock, yes. He is the source of life, yes. He is the reason for our existence, yes. But in addition to our relationship with God, we are created to be in community with people. We need helpers.

A lesser known fact about me: I am the world's worst fisherman. That's not hyperbole. My dad, who really is a pretty good fisherman, has taken me fishing many times over the years. I've trolled for trout, angled for bass, jigged for salmon, and even cast a few flies. I love the idea of fishing, but when I move beyond the idea, when I move past theory, one thing has always eluded me. One thing has always kept me from enjoying it the way my dad does, the way almost everyone who fishes enjoys it: the fish. I don't catch any.

I don't know why this is, and it doesn't make any sense to me because fishing isn't hunting. You don't have to stalk a salmon or cover yourself with trout urine so they don't smell you, and despite the admonitions of every early morning fishing trip, I am even skeptical that you have to keep all that quiet.

While diehard fishermen may disagree with me, success in fishing seems to be largely about preparation and equipment. The right lure, spot, time, technique, and voila, a fish is on the line. Equipment impacts hunting, but a good hunter can be largely successful with inferior equipment. On the other hand, while there is definitely skill involved in scouting, casting, reeling, and netting, all the skill in the world won't make fish bite the wrong lure if you are in the wrong place at the wrong time.

That's what doesn't make sense about my inability to catch fish. I'll be on a boat with another well-intentioned but prideful fisherman who is determined to show me that the curse is nonsense. We'll be fishing at the same time, in the same spot, using the same equipment, and the fish just don't bite my line. It is a mystery. And while I don't know why it is, I do know when it started.

When I was nine or ten, my family took a trip to Alaska. No, we didn't fly. We drove, towing a trailer thirty-five miles per hour on a 2,000-mile dirt road. Sound fun? That trip produced more stories than I can relate in this book, from forest fires to car crashes to falling rocks to air sickness to grizzly bears. I remember much of this trip with absolute clarity, and it was a very long trip. Over sixty hours of drive time on that dirt road tested our resolve as a family.

But one of the things that made the trip ok was the fishing. It was great. Nearly forty years later, I still remember reeling in the grayling on rivers while being sucked dry by the biggest mosquitos you will ever see. At that point in my life, I was still a normal kid when it came to fishing. Sometimes I caught fish, and some-times I didn't.

It all changed when we reached the Kenai River. The river literally boiled with fish. That's no joke. The salmon were so thick it looked like you could walk across the water on their backs. We weren't there long, but it seemed like a never-ending parade of men coming back with salmon. My dad caught one that was nearly as big as I was, and I wanted to go out on the river so badly. But I was young, and the boat was full, so while the men and older boys fished, I sat.

I waited for my turn. And waited. And waited. Eventually, sooner rather than later, the patience of a nine-year-old boy runs out. So, probably after about twenty minutes, I decided that I would take my fate in my own hands. I figured that if they weren't going to take me out, I'd do it myself.

It was the middle of the day, and no one was out fishing at the time. I desperately wanted to catch a big fish like my dad, so I grabbed a pole, geared up, and got in the boat alone.

Of course, I wasn't going anywhere. The boat was tied to the dock, and I didn't know how to start or drive it anyway. The men snickered a bit at the adorable ignorance of a nine-year-old thinking the fish would swim up to the dock to be caught. I have come to believe that this amusement is a side effect of a disease that you catch if you fish too long. I call it the I've-fished-so-long-I-forgot-that-fish-really-do-have-to-swim-up-and-bite-my-lure-itis.

So, I sat defiantly in the boat and cast the line from my salmon pole out into the river in hopes of hooking a "big one." Unfortunately, that is exactly what happened. I had reeled in a couple of times and then cast out again, when, all of a sudden, the pole started making this horrible whining noise as the line shot out of the reel. It was terrifying. First, because I thought that high-pitched whining sound was some kind of air raid siren for the nuclear war that we all knew was imminent in 1982, but then I was even more scared because I realized that I had hooked a big salmon and had no clue what to do with it.

I reminded myself that I was the son of football coach. I was growing into a man. I was a red-blooded American male in the throes of a primal and manly pursuit. Be a man, Joel! So, I screamed for my daddy! But as my dad and the others came running, the salmon ignored my ineptitude, and the line screamed almost as loudly as I had as it continued to shoot down the river.

The men looked at me with disbelief. They froze for a second. They battled with the instinctive celebration that is always produced by a fish on the line and the incongruent injustice of landing a whopper from a boat tied to the dock. They looked at me with the combination of pride and jealousy that you only see in fishermen when someone has a really big fish on the line, a really big fish.

But while they were trying to reconcile their worth as men, the line just kept going.

Eventually, they came to their senses, jumped in the boat, and while they were getting it untied and the motor started, my dad yelled, "Reel! Joel! Reel it in!"

But I was frozen. I was literally petrified with fear.

Instead of reeling, I pleaded, "You do it, Dad!" Not because I couldn't do it; I had fished before. I was prepared. I had the right equipment. I clearly had the right time and place. And even though the pole was way too big for me and the salmon reel was so heavy that it flipped upside down, making me reel it on the left-hand side, I knew what to do. I just didn't *want* to do it. I was scared. I wanted my dad to do it for me.

Now, forty years later, I understand what my dad was likely processing while I was dealing with my own anxiety: This is a big moment for my son. This is really cool. There is an opportunity for him to catch a really big fish. If I do this for him, I take that opportunity from him. The value here isn't in owning a dead fish. It is in *catching* it. If I catch it for him, he gains nothing. He just needs some encouragement.

So, he said, "No, son. You can do it. Just reel it in." And that broke the spell. Armed with the encouragement and confidence that comes from your father believing in you, I hefted the pole under my armpit and started reeling. I reeled with everything I had. I reeled until I literally couldn't reel anymore. *Literally*, because in relatively short order, the handle detached from the reel. It turns out that with the pole upside down and with me reeling with my left hand, I was actually reeling backward. No one noticed as the line continued to fly down the river until I unscrewed the arm off of the reel.

I held up the handle to my dad with the betrayed, accusatory, helpless expression that all fathers get from their children at some point, and then we both watched the line reach its terminus. Zzzeeeeeeeeeeeee, plink! It was over. The fish, the one that literally got away, ran the entire line out of the reel.

And that's where my run of bad luck started. From that point on, I have been criminally bad at catching fish.

I was pretty mad at my dad in the moment, but the anger was short-lived. Ultimately, it was sourced in my pride, not my father. I had missed a chance at catching a fish and showing the men that I could do it. As I said, it didn't last long because, later, when I looked back at it, I realized that my dad was there. It wasn't his fault the reel broke. He couldn't have known. He tried to help. He believed in me. And he was *with* me.

The full verse of Genesis 2:18 says, "Then the Lord God said, 'It is not good that the man should be alone; I will make him a helper fit for him.'" I couldn't stay mad at my dad because he was my helper. A helper is not a master or servant. A helper is someone who lightens your load and allows you to do something that you may not have the ability, commitment, desire, or talent to do on your own. My dad was providing me with the help I needed. He thawed me out of my frozen fear and snapped me into action. Taking the reel would not have been helping; it would have been doing. And we were not created with a deep desire for others to do for us. We don't need doers. We need helpers.

If you have ever lifted weights with the express goal of increasing your strength, you probably understand this concept. Many people go into the gym, begin picking up weights, and push and pull them around. They sweat and exert themselves to one degree or another, and to some degree, this is beneficial. For the most part, even unfocused strength training creates benefits for the participant. But if you truly want to make progress and get stronger, you need a partner. You need a spotter.

A good spotter has experience with you. He knows your abilities, limits, and, importantly, knows your goals (long-term or immediate). They pay close attention to you as you approach your moment of failure. This is the critical role of the spotter. He knows what you are trying to accomplish. He knows the pain you are going through, and before you fail, the spotter provides the support you need so you can complete the exercise.

Outside of just walking away and leaving you with a heavy weight, there are two mistakes that bad spotters make. First, they wait too long to help. They allow you to fail to the point where you are too exhausted to finish. This isn't all bad, but it limits the benefit from the exercise. If the spotter steps in too late, the result is an inability to continue for the time being.

The second mistake is worse; the spotter steps in too much. The spotter helps to a degree that you don't struggle with the weight. This spotter adds very little value because he is keeping you from doing the very thing you set out to do—struggle to achieve growth.

Like my dad or my wife, a good helper walks alongside. She doesn't step in to take the pain away but to make it bearable because life is like a gym you can never leave. There will always be struggle and pain.

Psychological, emotional, or physical pain exists, and it exists along a fairly broad spectrum of discomfort, anxiety, annoyance, ache, terror, or agony. It exists and cannot be eliminated without eliminating life itself. It exists and is a warning of potential harm. What causes pain can result in injury or death, but it can also result in growth, strength, wisdom, and compassion. But we have very little ability to discern the potential outcome of the episodes of pain in our lives. We just don't know, especially when we are in the midst of it. Pain overwhelms our ability to step back from the situation and gain perspective. It exists, and avoiding it only leaves you weak, flabby, immature, and more susceptible to the next episode of pain in your life. So, it is not a question of whether it exists but of how you navigate it, learn from it, come out of it on the other side, or how you prepare for the next episode of pain.

In living my life, I am not looking for others to do it for me. It is my life, situation, pain, and growth. A helper that takes that from me takes away all the bad—the fear, pain, and failure, but he also takes from me the opportunity for growth, success, relief, healing, and achievement.

The book of Genesis points out that it is not good for us to lift the weight alone. We may be able to do it. We may be able to get through it, but there is a vast chasm between adequate and good, and while you may be able to adequately go through life alone, it is not good to do so. For life to be good, we need suitable helpers. We need community: helpers, spotters, friends, lovers, brothers, sisters, parents, and neighbors. We need people who know us and our limits. We need people who are walking through life with us. We need people who are not *in* the struggle because that allows them to give us perspective *on* the struggle. We need people who will just be there with us when the line breaks.

Chapter 6

Comfort and Strength

When my daughter was eight, she broke her arm riding her bike. Like many people, she lost control of the bike and threw her arm out to catch herself. Pain. Tears. Fear. It was one of those moments that parents dread. My daughter looked up at me and wanted me to fix it. It hurt. It was serious. She had real need. She expected her daddy to make it better, and there was nothing I could do about it.

I knew that her life was not in danger, but I also knew that she was suffering, and I knew the pain would not stop for a while. I knew that the best thing I could do was to immobilize it and get her to a doctor. In other words, I knew that what I should not do was exactly what she was counting on me to do. I should not try and fix it.

My daughter looked at me and cried out. I wanted to comfort her. I wanted to take away the pain. I wanted to make it so it never happened, but I felt powerless. So I held her, tried to calm her, and I took her to the doctor. I sat with her. I talked with her. I agreed with her that it hurt and that I too wished it hadn't happen. I waited with her through the questions, forms, and x-rays. We waited together for the painkillers to kick in to offer her a little comfort from the pain, but that isn't what painkillers do, is it? Painkillers don't offer comfort at all.

Ok, so maybe they do in the more modern sense of the word, like a bed is comfortable or how I find comfort in a cup of hot cocoa. In our culture, comfort has come to mean the reduction or deadening of pain, but I've learned that that isn't really what comfort is. That is more what comfort does. Comfort lessens or make bearable, but defining a word by saying what it does is like defining the word dog by saying it barks. Comfort does make pain easier to endure, but what *is* it?

It is an interesting word, comfort. It comes from the two Latin roots of com and fortis. The fort part is pretty easily understood without any Latin background. Fort has remained an English word today. It is a place of strength. Fortis means strong.

Com, though, is a bit more indirect, even though we use words like comfort in the English language all the time without really thinking about it: compassion, companion, community, comfort. Com is a Latin root that means with or together. So, if you look up the definition of compassion in the dictionary, you will get something like feeling deep sorrow for someone else; it's more direct meaning is to suffer *with* (passion comes from the Latin for suffer). If I have compassion for you, I suffer *with* you. A companion is someone who you "eat *with*" (panis means bread). So, comfort (with and strength) is to be strong together, or maybe it is better stated as the strength you receive by being *with* someone.

Saying that comfort is the lessening of pain is like saying courage is the lessening of fear. It is close but not a very complete description. Courage doesn't remove fear; it provides the ability to overcome fear. Fear is lessened in its relative status compared to your ability to deal with it, but the presence of courage does not eliminate the presence of fear. If the presence of fear is removed, then the presence of courage is also removed. You cannot be courageous unless you are also afraid. Courageous people have a high ability to overcome their fear. In a way, for courageous people, fear is lessened, but it would miss the point to say that courage *is* the lessening of fear. The lessening of fear is the *result* of courage, not courage itself.

In the same way, comfort isn't the lessening of pain. The lessening of pain is the *result* of comfort in that comfort allows for a higher ability to deal with pain, and like courage, if the presence of pain is eliminated then the presence of comfort is as well. Comfort is the strength you receive from someone else that allows you to overcome the pain in your life.

The painkillers didn't offer my daughter comfort per se. Painkillers synthesize the outcome of comfort. Painkillers reduce the impact of pain without increasing your tolerance for it. Tylenol doesn't give comfort; it attempts to make you not experience what is really there. No one receives strength from ibuprofen. Comfort doesn't remove the pain; it makes you strong enough to endure it. And that strength comes from being "with" one another.

Think of it in terms of physical strength. If I were to walk over to a pull-up bar in my current condition, I may be able to do five pull-ups. By the end, I would be really straining, and there would be a degree of pain involved in the exercise. The act of pulling myself up results in me raising my chin above the bar several times. If I continue to do this, presumably, over time, I would be able to do more pull-ups than I could at the beginning. Working by myself, monitoring my own ability, and dealing with the pain by myself, I should be able to make progress, but that progress is likely to be slow. My motivation, my desire to push a little further waxes and wanes from day to day, yet, no matter my motivation, when I get to number five, I have no ability to get to number six by myself.

A good workout partner helps a lot. She can encourage or rebuke me when I get down on myself and feel like quitting. She can lend me some strength when I am failing and allow me to get to six or seven pull-ups rather than the five I can do on my own. With the help of a partner, I can grow stronger more quickly and increase my ability to overcome the weight of my existence.

I could use a synthetic helper that allowed me to not feel the weight from my body, maybe some kind of pulley system that lifts my body up and down several times. The problem is that this system is, at best, attempting to remove a portion of my weight or, at worst, lifting me to the top of the bar with no effort at all. The first helps but only reduces the effort down to my current ability. Even if I am very careful about its use, I still run into the problem of my fluctuating motivation and desire, let alone days that I am simply weaker, more tired, or injured. This scenario is less ideal than the human partner, but the second scenario actually makes me weaker.

If I remove too much resistance, I accomplish the outcome of the exercise but lose the benefit. I move my chin above the bar repeatedly, but, over time, I lose strength, and if the pulley system ever breaks down, I find that I can't lift my body at all, let alone the five times I started with.

The problem with this analogy is that exercise is something you opt into. You do not have to exercise today. You opt into it. You opt into pain in order to get stronger. But the pain of life is not something we opt into. It is inevitable. You can't avoid it. Life is more like having your hands permanently attached to the pull-up bar with food and water on a shelf above it.

If I know I cannot walk away from pain and it will inevitably and consistently return, then there are real consequences for cheating the system. A synthetic system of exercise not only risks muscle atrophy but also weight gain. I may lose the strength I have while simultaneously requiring more strength to lift myself up for the next meal.

Trying to navigate life by avoiding all occurrences of pain is eventually crippling, but so is trying to do it on your own. We all need helpers. We all need more strength than we possess. We all need comfort.

From the time I could drive, I always wanted a Jeep. I am not sure what the draw was. I'm not really an off-road type of guy. I don't ride motorcycles or ATVs, but I've always been drawn to the old CJs of the late 70's and early 80s. The problem is that I am an almost obsessively value-driven person when it comes to money. So, when I was eighteen and I went to the dealership to buy my first car, I didn't drive away with a Jeep. The salesperson would not come down on the price, so when I gave up on the negotiation, we chatted for several minutes. I found out that he had graduated a few years earlier from the same high school, and I learned that he had his eye on a sweet, blue, 1986 BMW 325 (with an installed car phone!). It had sat in the lot for almost thirty days, and nobody was buying. He told me that if it didn't sell soon, he could buy it for slightly above cost, which he also shared with me (which was well below the price on the windshield), and low and behold, it turned out, that while they wouldn't budge on the Jeep, the BMW, *at cost*, was in my price range.

Even now, I tell this story with a mixture of pride and shame. I had no intention of buying a BMW. I wanted a Jeep, but I couldn't get the Jeep in the budget I set for myself. So, I came back the next day and bought the BMW from a different person for slightly above cost.

I enjoyed driving that car for six or seven years. It was an absolutely great car to drive. I loved my BMW, but I never stopped wanting a Jeep. So, in 1998, when it was time to buy again, I got a Toyota Camry (check my man card at the door).

It had good gas mileage, high safety ratings, was priced affordably, appropriate for the family I was anticipating starting with my wife and was known to be incredibly reliable. It was a very reasonable purchase and probably about as far away from a 1979 CJ than you can get. But I knew that I was likely to almost never have problems with it. It was a high-value proposition. Like I said, it was extremely reliable, too reliable.

Seventeen years later, in 2015, I was still driving that Camry. Despite my best efforts at running it into the ground, that car was bullet proof. But I still wanted a

Jeep, so in the fall of 2015, when I was rear-ended, and the Camry was totaled, I finally did it. Regardless of value, I made myself buy a Jeep.

I bought a 2010 Jeep Wrangler Unlimited Sahara. It was not exactly the CJ of my dreams—automatic transmission, stock, road tires, and no lift, but I finally had one. I told myself that I could modify it later, but for now, I had a Jeep! Trail-rated! There was no stopping me now. I felt like I could conquer whatever nature threw at me.

That winter, I was driving home with my ten-year-old daughter, and as we turned onto our long gravel driveway, I let her drive. She sat on my lap and worked the steering wheel as I worked the pedals. We drove up our long driveway and veered off onto the access road that runs up behind our house. My backyard opens up into a small field, so we drove up to it to turn around. We weren't really full-blown, off-roading, and rock-crawling in a lifted all-terrain monster, but it kind of felt like it (in a ten-year-old girl and forty-three-year-old, middle aged, fixed-income manager kind of way).

We came to the end of the road and began to turn around in the field when we just stopped moving. The rear wheels began spinning, but there was no forward momentum. Adrenalin shot through me. I lifted Halle off my lap, jammed it into four-wheel drive and trusted my trail-rated, go anywhere, do anything Jeep to pull me back to solid ground. I eased the gas pedal and slowly began to move... lower into the mud.

As my highway-rated, go to work, just do your job Jeep spun its tires, it sunk up to the axles in the mud of my backyard. If you are human, you have probably felt as I did at that moment. I was embarrassed, worried, and angry all at the same time. I wanted to blame someone. As ridiculous as it was, I wanted it to be my daughter's fault. I knew it wasn't, but I was still short-tempered with her. I wanted it to be Fiat's fault—stupid Italian company ruining an American legend. Who puts road tires and an automatic transmission on a Jeep?! They'd only do that if enough idiots were buying Jeeps this way (people like me! Aaaarrrrggggghhhh!).

Somebody needed to be blamed here. My Jeep was stuck in the mud! It's a friggin' Jeep! It isn't supposed to get stuck in the mud, at least not in this kind of mud. I'm not off-roading in the mountains. I'm one hundred feet away from my back door!

I desperately wanted it to be someone else's fault, someone besides me, but I couldn't come up with a villain. At best, I should have known more. I should have known that the ground was saturated from late autumn rains. I should have had it in four-wheel drive. I shouldn't have had my daughter on my lap. But it sounded hollow. I couldn't have reasonably foreseen any of it. This was just an accident; just one of those crummy things that happen. The real problem, though, was that despite not finding anyone to blame, it was really embarrassing. I didn't want to tell anyone. I felt emasculated.

Of course, my wife came out. To her credit, she looked at me processing these feelings in real time and quickly wiped the smirk off her face. She could tell that I didn't think it was funny (even though it was. It was really funny. My 4,000-pound SUV was up to its axels in mud in my back yard). But she is a good woman, and she could tell that I was not able to see the humor yet. So, she told me to call my friends to come help.

My wife is a good woman, yes, but so naïve. She didn't get it. There was no way I was going to call my friends and open myself up to ridicule. No one would believe this was anything but operator error, and operator error in a Jeep (or power tool or home remodeling) is basically the same thing as saying, "masculine malfunction." I may as well check my man card at the door again and trade my Jeep in for a Fiat. Instead, I changed my clothes and grabbed a shovel. I spent the next two hours digging, wedging boards under the tires, and trying to make some kind of progress. In the end, I was rewarded with a sore back and exhaustion but no change in the situation. I just couldn't get that stupid Jeep out of the mud by myself.

Have I mentioned that my wife is a good woman? She brought me some Gatorade and gently suggested

I call my friends again. But, of course, I refused. There was no way I would call my friends.

I texted them. Twenty minutes later, my Jeep was out of the mud, and I was cleaning the mud out of the wheels. My friend Kevin lived ten minutes away and came over with his diesel Ford F250. He backed his truck up, and we hooked a chain to his hitch and my front bumper. I got into the Jeep and eased on the gas as Kevin did the same. It literally took longer to hook up the chain than to pull me out of the mud. It was comically easy. A little help, and my Jeep popped right out of the mud like it wasn't even stuck.

Two hours of self-reliant, hard labor resulted in no progress whatsoever. Ten minutes of assistance resulted in freedom from the mire (there might be a lesson in there somewhere). That isn't to say that self-reliance is a bad thing or that I need assistance with everything in my life. If my wife were to place her hand over mine and help me brush my teeth every morning, it would more likely result in bleeding gums than clean teeth, but we all run into situations that are simply beyond our ability or, maybe more importantly, ineffective to overcome on our own. In those instances, we need others to lend their strength. We need comfort, the strength that comes from being with others.

Sometimes, many times, we aren't strong enough on our own, and the presence, assistance, and partnership of others in our lives makes us stronger. I think we operate with the wrong notion of comfort, that comfort implies a softness in our lives. But comfort no more implies softness than courage implies safety. We think of comfort in terms of a cushioned mattress. Come to think of it, maybe that is correct.

Anyone who has slept on an old, broken-down mattress understands the point here. Sleeping on the hard ground can cause pain and aches, so we buy a mattress to support our bodies above the ground. It is the mattress's strength that provides comfort. When that mattress breaks down and loses its strength, it stops working as well. We lose the comfort that the mattress provides.

The book of Ecclesiastes addresses this as well: "Two are better than one, because they have a good reward for their toil. For if they fall, one will lift up his fellow. But woe to him who is alone when he falls and has not another to lift him up! Again, if two lie together, they keep warm, but how can one keep warm alone? And though a man might prevail against one who is alone, two will withstand him—a threefold cord is not quickly broken" (4:9–12)[12].

To deny that you will invariably come up against something in your life that is greater than your ability alone is folly. It is arrogance, ignorance, or delusion. Furthermore, to keep bull-headedly digging when your life is stuck in the mud may make you stronger and save your pride, but if you never accept the help of others, all you are doing is digging your own grave.

Which brings me back to football. Football is especially dear to me because of the complexity of the game. There are simply too many factors for anyone's individual strength and confidence to carry the team. Contrary to sports media journalists, even a great quarterback cannot do this. Put a good quarterback on a bad team, and you have a bad team with a good quarterback. More often than not, what happens is not that the team gets better but that the quarterback gets worse because his confidence erodes. Give a good team a bad coach, and they will still win, but probably win less. Give a bad team to a good coach, and they may win more, but it won't turn them around. Any way you slice it, football is a sport where everyone must depend on others for success. The coach can come up with the best game plan and strategy, but he needs his assistants to implement it and players to execute it. A quarterback may throw the perfect pass, but the receiver still needs to catch it. The defense may stop the other team, but they still need their offense to score to win the game. And the kicker... Well, never mind, that may be going too far.

All joking aside, football simply doesn't work without an inordinate amount of people working together for the same purpose. Even at the highest levels of football, the game functions with around twenty-five starting players. The game is exhausting, violent, long, and operates with the added complexity of placing coaches that are separate from the play, observing, strategizing, and manipulating the movements on the field in real time.

The game is too large to be played effectively by generalists, so over time, football has developed more specialized responsibilities and positions. While you can make a case for theoretically creating the perfect athlete for many sports and playing that athlete at every position, you cannot do so in football. In general, I can conceive of five basketball players (say five clones of Lebron James) playing effective and winning basketball. That doesn't mean that this fictitious team would win every game or wouldn't be susceptible to certain lineups or teams. It is just to say that this team would be effective. No position on the court is so specialized that Lebron James couldn't play it. And for the most part, this is true of most other team sports.

Clone Derrick Jeter, Wayne Gretzky, or Messi and play them at each position, and you generally have effective teams. The obvious exceptions come at the specialized positions: goal keeper, catcher, pitcher, goal tender. But for the most part, the same ideal player can play everywhere in most sports. In football this doesn't work. Walter Payton cannot effectively play quarterback, offensive line, corner, or defensive end. Tom Brady cannot play linebacker. Jerry Rice cannot play defensive tackle. Cloning an outstanding football player would actually create a bad football team.

Football can't be generalized. The challenge is too great for individuals to overcome. In football, as in life, individuals can impact the outcome for brief moments in time but cannot direct the outcome of a game over extended periods. As with life, there is no one set of skills or abilities that prepares you for all that you are to confront. Football requires a team with members of varying abilities and attributes. Playing on a team allows even the strongest athlete to accomplish something they are unable to do on their own, and so, playing on a team is also uniquely effective at revealing your weaknesses.

Throwing a ball in my backyard, I can believe that I'm a good quarterback. I can believe I am fast and strong. I can convince myself that I can do everything well. This becomes much harder to do as I join a team and begin to compete. The larger the team and scope of my competition, the more I find out that what I thought was good simply isn't. My limited perception of goodness was actually awkward, slow, and weak when compared to the greatness that is possible. The only way to be content with that level of performance is to refuse inclusion of others into your team.

If I want to succeed and play the game at the highest level, I must surround myself with those who can be trusted to provide comfort (strength with) when needed. I must have teammates worthy of my faith in them because "faith is confidence in what we hope for and assurance about what we do not see" (Heb. 11:1[13]).

For strength produces hope, faith is the confidence in what is hoped for, and life is way bigger than football or muddy backyards.

We cannot hope to overcome it on our own. The truly successful person is one who endures, perseveres, and develops his own strength while recognizing his limitations and need for others. He must surround himself with a group of faithful people. For those challenges that life will throw at us that dwarf our individual and isolated strength, we need comfort.

But comfort does not eliminate the pain of our circumstances. It doesn't take the mud away or keep us from ever getting stuck. Comfort is the strength we lend to those we love when they experience the pain of life, and while we usually refer to comfort as physical in nature, like a mattress or chain and a truck, just as pain is often emotional or psychological, comfort is as well.

When Kari's father passed away, I would have eliminated that pain if I could have. I would have brought him back to life and restored him to health, but I do not have that power. None of us do. Instead, I lent her my strength. I comforted her. It didn't take her pain away. I may have been tempted to give her false hope by saying something like, "It's going to be alright," but that isn't comfort. It wasn't going to be alright. Losing a father is real, painful, and permanent. There is no "fixing" it. There is only coping with it. To imply that this was temporary would just be denying the truth of the pain.

I may have offered plausible hope about seeing him someday in heaven, and while that is a helpful truth and may offer some relief, it isn't the extent of what was needed. The loss she felt was painful in the moment, and the strength she needed was for the present. All I could do was be "with" her in her pain by being there, an arm around the shoulder, a listening ear. Because comfort is a "with" thing. It doesn't take the pain away; it makes it more bearable, because what makes pain more bearable is having someone else in it with you. There is no comfort in solitude, but there is strength in numbers.

CHAPTER 7

LIVE, LOVE, HOPE

THE PROBLEM WITH life, as I see it, is that we are strong enough to exist by ourselves but not strong enough to live. In general, I can make it through whatever life throws at me. I can lower my head and focus on the challenge before me. I can persevere. I can outlast.

I take pride in my ability to withstand the pain of life, and I don't think I'm alone there. We love movies like *Rocky* or *Rudy*. We love stories where the protagonist is tougher than the overwhelming odds stacked against him. We love stories of endurance like *Unbroken*, tales of an unbreakable determination to make it through. Mind over matter. Resilience. Strength.

There is a trap there, though. These stories assume that there is life bookending the struggle, that there was life before and that there will be life after the story is told. The victory achieved in these tales is one of reclaiming that life that was in jeopardy or one of attaining the opportunity for a better life. We may have stopped ending stories with "and they lived happily ever after", but we have never stopped wishing it to be true. Well-loved movies of struggle have an implied payoff of a life full of joy and fulfillment, because we all want that payoff. I want the love of a girl. I want the admiration of my friends and family. I want the recognition of my teammates. I want freedom to live my life as I choose. And I am willing to persevere to get it; I am willing to fight and struggle and sacrifice. I'll take anything Apollo Creed can throw at me, and I'll still be standing. I can take a punch. I can lower my head and outlast.

The trap is that life is not a story within a larger story. At the end of the story of life, Rocky doesn't walk away with pride and a life with Adrian. Rudy doesn't get carried off the field. Louie Zamperini doesn't return to a life of freedom. At the end of the stories of our lives, we die.

You can't outlast life. Getting through, persevering, getting to the next round... that just isn't good enough. When life itself is the challenge, there is no payoff at the end. The payoff of life is not in reaching the end of it but in living each moment along the way.

Kari and I have taken the family to Disneyland twice. Sometimes I remember those trips and want to go back again. Sometimes. As a parent of four kids, it is undeniable that there are parts of Disneyland that are terrific. Disney takes the fantastic world of their animated movies and transforms it into real life in a clean, organized, and approachable way. Watching your four-year-old walk up to Mickey Mouse while battling her internal fear and wonder or sitting next to your giggling child as she "wahoos" on a ride truly brings joy to a parent's heart. On the other hand, spending hours in line entertaining four children with twenty-five-dollar toys and sixteen-dollar corn dogs in between running for Fast Passes through 500 acres filled with thousands of potential pedophiles is a father's worst nightmare.

At Disneyland, my focus as a father quickly shifts from enjoying the happiest place on earth with my children to accomplishing the goals:

1. We need to see all the attractions (I had to mortgage the house to bring a family of six here, and we are going to get our money's worth).
2. We need to maintain a minimum level of nutrition without taking out a second mortgage (Ok. Eighteen-dollar chicken strips for Jack... By my count, he just threw away twelve dollars of chicken strips. I could probably fish those out of the garbage... Never mind. I just won't eat).
3. Get everyone home safely (Oh sh%t! Where's Halle?!).
4. And, oh yeah. Pins! We need to exchange pins (What?! Why do we want to do that?!).

If you have been there with your kids, you know of what I speak. Disneyland is the happiest place on earth for some. For the rest of us, it is lunacy; a mental state cycling between anxiety, manic joy, terror, and depression (emotional *and* economic).

As parents, we see all the risks and repercussions that our children do not see. I see debt, kidnapping, exhaustion, and nausea. My daughter sees Cinderella. My perspective and experience show me all the things that can go wrong. My son's lack of experience shows him that this is where Buzz Lightyear lives. I focus on surviving. They focus on living.

After two trips to Disneyland with my kids, I learned that you must be very careful and disciplined during experiences like these. If you are not, you will look back at the pictures of your smiling kids and your frowning face and realize you missed the joy that was right in front of you. The happiness of life flowed around you like a rock in a river while you focused on everything that could go wrong. The innocence of your children's younger years disappeared as you concerned yourself with their lack of fear.

It is not enough to just get through life. Yes, sometimes there are short-term challenges that need to be overcome. Sometimes you need to wait in line for Magic Mountain, but no one goes to Disneyland so they can stoically wait in line. You wait in line so you can *experience* Disneyland, and if you are going to have to wait in line, don't you want to do it with someone else? Isn't waiting in line alone the worst kind of waiting in line? And if you are going to wait in line with someone, isn't it is much better to play "I spy" with your kids while you are doing it?

Sometimes you need to put in the work to get to the next ride, but if you are not careful, all of life becomes a series of sprints for Fast Passes, and even while you are on the ride, you can't enjoy it because you are already worried about the next thing. Soon the lines become indistinguishable from the rides.

So, to enjoy Disneyland, you must savor the experiences as they come, but there is one more lesson you learn at the happiest place on earth. If you are there for the rides alone, you will be sorely disappointed. The rides are fun, but at Disneyland, as in life, you will spend significantly more time in line than you will on the rides. The joy of the experience then, comes not only from the rides themselves, but what we do in between the rides, and life is so much bigger than Disneyland.

The time in between those peak moments of excitement is so much longer than the moments themselves, and our time is limited. Knowing that, we must make the most of the time we have. We must *live*, not merely exist. We must squeeze life for what it has to offer, not just get through it, or at the end of our time, we will exit the park with nothing but debt and regret.

The problem, of course, is that life is constantly throwing things at us that get in the way of our enjoyment of it: sickness, injury, depression, anxiety, poverty, hunger, loneliness... pain. At times, life can seemingly be a never ending series of trials, but for many of us, we know that we are strong enough to get through them. We know that we can fight the pain till another moment of reprieve comes. We can persevere, and when the latest trial passes, we will get back to living. The line will end. We can wait it out.

Be honest. Look back on your life. How much of your life is made up of "getting through"? How much time do you spend in your job waiting for vacation or retirement? How much television do you watch to pass the time? How much do you drink to forget the past, even at the expense of forgetting the present along with it? How often have you looked back and thought, "Where did the time go?" How many times have you wished you could do it over and be more present with your kids, spouse, or parents?

Getting through is not good enough. Waiting for the wait to end or the pain to cease is about as effective as leaving the milk on the counter so it can freshen up. There are realities with which we must come to grips. There are facts we simply must accept, whether or not we believe they should be true.

Life is full of pain. Denying it doesn't make it go away. Diminishing the pain in our lives based on some absolute scale, comparison to other's pain, or some theoretical or potential pain doesn't make it less real. In addition to the very real existence of personal pain in all our lives is the uncomfortable reality that some pain is necessary or good for us. We don't grow without pain. In fact, we are not just less likely to grow if we are sheltered from pain; we are likely to atrophy and die. This is the great catch-22 of life: Pain exists. It sucks. But we need it.

For most of us, we inherently understand this situation. We practice it, exercise, and strive. We learn to cope. And maybe because we instinctively connect growth and strength to overcoming pain in our lives, we default to handling it on our own. We put our heads down and endure it. We get through.

But pain, in one form or another, does not end. There are reprieves, yes, but to believe that everyone, absolutely everyone on this planet does not experience pain and will not experience pain again in the future many times is delusional. Ignoring it won't make it go away, and it won't make it stop coming back. Waiting, getting through, and ignoring the reality of life only squanders what little of it we have. So rather than waiting for the end, rather than waiting in line by oneself, choose to ask someone to wait with you.

Whether it is waiting for a ride at Disneyland, tickets to a concert, or at the DMV, waiting in line is simply better if someone is willing to do it with you. Of course, there's the rub; it is incredibly awkward to ask someone to wait in line with you. It is one thing if they are obligated or happen to be waiting in line for the same thing, but assuming they have an option not to wait in line and have to opt in to waiting with you; it is worse than walking across the seventh-grade auditorium over to a group of girls to ask out Heather Stimpleton. It is risky, vulnerable, awkward, and mortifying.

When you ask someone to wait in line with you, you do so in full knowledge that no one likes to wait in line. There is no club of line-waiters for people who seek out long lines on the weekend for the joy of waiting in them. In fact, there are whole industries built around allowing people to skip the line, to shorten the wait: fast food, delivery, Amazon, TSA PreCheck, and, of course, Fast Passes. People will pay significantly and accept lower quality to skip the line. The only reason we wait in line is that the payoff at the end of the line is necessary or worth it.

To ask someone to wait with you in a line, to be with you in your pain, acknowledges that the only reason they would do so would be out of love for you. (Oh. That got really uncomfortable.) It might not be romantic love or even strong love. It may be brotherly or neighborly love, but it is love because no one will wait in line with you in the absence of love. To wait in line with someone, you have to care about him enough to place his interest above your own, or you have to enjoy his company enough to subjugate yourself to the pain you do not want to be in.

Either way, inviting someone into your life like this is, in some way, a referendum on your value. Rejection by a line-waiting companion is at least in part a rejection of you, and that is another reason why we often choose to wait alone. I would much rather experience loneliness than couple it with rejection.

To invite someone in is, as people like to say, to "put yourself out there." It is literally stepping out and laying yourself bare, even to a small degree, for someone else to see your weakness, your need. "Putting yourself out there" is like allowing a giant light to shine upon the reality of your situation. You are in pain and don't want to do it alone. You'd like them to comfort you. To put yourself out there, to step out of the shadows and into the light, to stop pretending that you are strong enough can be terrifying. Allowing light to shine upon our weakness, flaws, failure, or rejection makes you vulnerable.

The light is scary,[14] and the darkness seems safe. Frankly, we love the darkness. Darkness promises to hide our shame and keep us safe. Darkness promises to limit our pain. Darkness promises a better life. Darkness lies.

Your shame is with you in the dark. Pain will find you whether you hide in the shadows or not. There is no security or safety in the dark. Darkness only obscures your vision; it does not change reality. The only chance you have at the life you want to lead is to step out into the light and live.[15]

When my son was young and playing baseball, I used to tell him, "You can't hit the ball if you don't swing." His problem was that he had defined failure for himself as striking out. He hated it. Striking out was embarrassing, so as his attention turned to avoiding the pain of striking out, he forgot the reason young boys play baseball in the first place: to hit the ball. They don't look forward to catching or even throwing it. They play to hit the ball. No one signs up for baseball with the eager anticipation of grinding out a walk.

I would explain to my son, "Son, if you don't swing, only two things can happen: you walk, or you strike out. And yes, I know getting on base is a good thing, and running the bases is better than going back to the dugout and sitting on the bench, but when we go out and play, do you ever say, 'Dad, let's go run bases?' No. You say, 'Dad, can we go hit?' Son, you like hitting. That's where the joy is. If you don't swing, you can't hit. If you don't swing, you will never experience the reason you play.

"If you don't swing, you either walk or strike out. On the other hand, if you swing, there are three possibilities: hit safely, hit and get out, or strike out. Yes, you can still get out if you hit the ball, but let's be honest, even hitting and getting out feels better than walking. After a game, you will talk to me about the groundball out or the pop fly that you just missed with more joy than any walk. So, bad things can happen if you swing, but good things can happen too.

"The really important part, though, the piece you really need to realize is that you can't eliminate the strikeout by not swinging. Keeping the bat on your shoulder only eliminates the joy of the game."

Remaining in line by yourself and just getting through life may seem safer, but staying in the dark will never eliminate the pain. It only eliminates the joy.

There is joy in sharing. By living with others, we don't only acquire strength but also joy. We make life better. The sensations and experiences of life, love, parenthood, adrenaline, hopes, and dreams all become brighter, deeper, and more poignant when shared.

You don't have to look further than your everyday life to see evidence of this: a good meal, a football game, a great bottle of wine, a good joke. I want another person to taste what I taste, to feel what I feel. Somehow, the wine is even more enjoyable in the company of someone else enjoying it alongside me. Experiencing an NBA playoff game alone or at the stadium; the two experiences aren't comparable. We love to cheer in crowds, to high-five strangers in the row below us. Watching a stand-up comic alone is funny. Watching that same comic with others is hysterical.

Shared life is simply better, but not just when life is good. Shared pain is better too. The death of a loved one, losing your job, the middle of the night and your daughter isn't home yet, depression—navigating these times with a spouse, close friend, or brother still hurts. It is painful, shameful, fearful, and sad. Going through them alone, though, is devastating.

Shared life offers us hope, hope in the strength to withstand a difficult and painful world, and hope for a life filled with joy. But to access that hope and joy and live a shared life, we must step into the light and invite someone in.

But even here, we try to hide in the shadows. Even in the invitation, I try to limit my exposure. I will invite someone on a very limited basis. I will try to use them for the strength or joy they may provide. I will try to keep it transactional.

"Here's the deal. I'll give you the opportunity to experience some of my life, and you give me your support. Sound good?" But this isn't sharing; it's using. It is giving something for the sake of getting something. Shared life is not a one-way street. It is not directional.

If I share a pizza with my wife, we both partake in the pizza. We sit down and each grab a slice or two (or three…). It isn't my pizza. It's our pizza. We are sharing it. Unfortunately, we use the same word when I share my fries with her, but then, I'm not really sharing. I give her a couple of fries, but I maintain ownership of the fries. They are mine (if you want more, get your own).

While sharing and giving are related, they are not the same thing. To give is directional. Giving abdicates ownership. It is directional, from me to you.

Sharing, however, is reciprocal. Sharing retains ownership but invites another party into that ownership as well. I don't share a pizza with my wife by giving her a slice. I share the pizza by giving up sole ownership of the pizza. We become co-owners in the whole. Furthermore, sharing assumes acceptance. If my wife refuses to eat the pizza, we are not sharing it.

Shared life assumes that someone else is willing to do just that: enter your life and participate in the whole. Shared life assumes that someone else walking through his own successes, failures, pain, confusion, and fear is willing to add walking through all those things with you as well. Who in his right mind would do that? What would motivate someone to voluntarily subject himself more risk, more pain?

That brings us back to love. It takes a shared love to join with someone else. It doesn't have to be romantic love. It can be love of a goal or endeavor. It can be the love of a friend. It can be the love of a spouse. It can be many different kinds of love, but it has to be love, which begs the question: What is love?

We throw this word around a lot in the English language—different kinds of love, love as a verb or noun, different degrees of love. Most definitions deal with passion, affection, or attraction, but I think this misses the mark. These are aspects of love but not the unique characteristic of love. The unique characteristic of love is related to where it places importance or value of a thing. Love exalts. Love places above.

I believe that for the vast majority of us and maybe all of us, we have a first love. Assuming a relatively healthy childhood, we all begin our lives loving ourselves. We see ourselves as special, exceptional, and worthy. At some point, this fades, but the fact remains that when a six-year-old believes he will be a professional athlete, he really believes it. He really thinks there is no reason he can't or already isn't the best at what he values.

Early in life, we exalt ourselves. As we grow, though, we find things outside ourselves to love. We begin to place others in that prime position. When love turns outside ourselves, it exalts that thing above our first love. What separates love from other forms of attraction is that it is selfless. Love necessarily places its object above the subject. "I love you" means, "I exalt you above me." Another way to say that is that love requires sacrifice.

If you are not willing to sacrifice for the person or thing you love, you simply do not have love. In fact, it isn't even about willingness. If you haven't sacrificed, you haven't loved. If your own needs, wants, and desires come before the object of your love, it isn't love. If you haven't seen it already, when you take a look at the essence of love, it is really a form of worship. You worship what you love.

I know this sounds overblown, but aside from the religious connotations of words like exalt and worship, this sacrificial desire, passion, or attraction can be tested easily in what we have witnessed in our own lives. Newlyweds, many times, abandon their own needs in pursuit of those of their new spouses. Young love is ripe with abuse of this reality, but that abuse also confirms the truth of its existence. Love demotes the lover. Love does not create an equal relationship. Love creates a servant relationship (which is why healthy relationships must have mutual love).

It isn't only with people. It can be with things or animals as well. Our pets, jobs, passions, purposes... for the things we love, we sacrifice. We serve them.

Asking someone to join you in line may be to join you in the pursuit of a business venture. Maybe it is to ask for companionship for a season of life, like your kid's soccer season. Maybe it is for a ministry. Regardless of what it is, to ask someone to join you in the line, to ask him to sacrifice his self-sufficiency, security, or time is to ask him if he loves a thing. Do you love this cause? Do you love this business? Do you love me?

Typing those words is almost cringeworthy. It feels vulnerable to ask those questions. And it is. It is incredibly vulnerable to lay your loves on the table and leave open to rejection the things you most value. It is incredibly vulnerable to step into the batter's box and swing, to step into the light, to step out of the false comfort of darkness. But you cannot find love in the dark.

Life is meant to be shared. It is better shared. We are stronger by sharing. We have hope through love and comfort. But we will never achieve these things unless we step into the light and let people see us.

CHAPTER 8

FRIENDS AND PARTNERS – STRENGTH FOR A SEASON

I HAVE NEVER been very good at friendship. For most of my life I have lived relying on myself to one degree or another. I probably need to go back to counseling to unpack that further, but let's just say that allowing myself to be relationally and emotionally vulnerable with other people has always been difficult. I simply don't feel safe doing so.

When I met my wife, I thought that would all change. I loved her like I had never loved anyone else. I wanted to share my entire self with her, but I soon figured out that doing so would also share the things that would hurt her. The fact of humanity is that each of us have a lot of junk that circulates in and around our heads and hearts—envy, lust, anger, insecurity, disgust, greed. No one is immune to these things. Everyone

– absolutely everyone – deals with really nasty stuff on a daily basis[16]. For the most part, we hold it back, but holding it back is not the same as it not existing. Is it?

Unfortunately, I'm pretty good at holding it back. I'm good at pretending. Compared to the population as a whole, most people would say I'm a fairly disciplined, moral person. They think I'm a good father and husband. They think I'm a good worker, member of my church, friend, citizen... But that is mainly because I figured out a trick while I was still young.

The key is not letting people get close. If you stay in the dark, they never see all the stuff you hold back, but that leads to a cold and arrogant existence. It is effective, but it isn't worth it.

Not being good at friendship doesn't mean I was a loner, though. Actually, I was always pretty popular in school. That was partly due to the fact that I was a fairly accepting kid. I'm sure there are people in my past who would disagree. I was a jerk at times. There was a time in my life that I was an adolescent boy (from about age ten to thirty-two), and I experienced all the self-centered, thoughtless, arrogant behaviors that go along with it. But, for the most part, I got along with almost everyone.

I think my popularity was also because I was a pretty high achiever. I was an athlete. I got good grades. I was funny (at least I thought so.) While I clearly wasn't the most attractive boy in school, I did all right. I wasn't really the best at anything, but I was always near the top in just about everything—the consummate A-/B+ student athlete. And, I was friendly. I liked to be liked. Who doesn't?

These qualities attracted people. Through my school years, there were always people around me, but like I said, I have never been very good with friends. I just didn't know what to do with them. Besides competing with them, entertaining them, or leading them, I didn't know how to *be with* them. All my relationships were directional, not reciprocal. I served others by helping or entertaining them. They served me in the same way. But there was no commitment toward each other or for a purpose or cause.

I just used people. It sounds terrible, but I think it was pretty normal. I don't think all the other kids were running around with intimate friendships while I was on the outside looking in. Much of my inability toward fostering real friendships was due to my age and the egocentric, self-centered worldview that virtually all teenagers exhibit.

But there were definitely some people who understood it. There were some genuine friendships among my peers. I say peers because I want to say friends, but they weren't friends, at least not in how I am defining friendship here. In my mind, there is a large gap between someone with whom you act friendly and a friend, just as there is a chasm between a person with whom you are neighborly and your neighbor.

It should be obvious in the word friendly. When you are friendly, you are acting *as if* the object of your actions is a friend. I will naturally be friendly with my friends, but I may be friendly to strangers as well. Just like the distinction in the definition of courage or comfort, there is a state of being in the definition of friend that goes beyond what it appears to be. Being friendly doesn't make you friends any more than showing love toward someone makes you lovers. You cannot just pretend. You have to commit, because the key ingredient to all lasting relationships (friendship, marriage, business partners) is commitment.

A shared life, for whatever reason it is shared, requires commitment toward sharing. It must be reciprocal rather than directional, and for that reciprocal relationship to be lasting or at least effective, both parties must be committed to what is being shared. And, of course, if both parties are committed to that sharing, the object of that sharing must be exposed to the light. You cannot commit to sharing something you keep hidden from the person with whom you are sharing. The difficulty is that the light comes largely after the commitment. It comes as a result of the commitment or at least simultaneously with the commitment. Regardless, commitment is key, and I simply didn't have it when I was younger.

For a large part of my life, I was too insecure to share myself with others. I could never tell if they were trustworthy or not, but I really wanted to trust someone with the things I wanted to do and be. I wanted to trust someone with my time and my *self*. So, I was friendly. I treated people well. I helped people. I entertained them. I worked hard. But I was also insecure, so I kept everyone at an arm's length.

I was essentially conducting a real-time, ongoing interview for my trust. I was constantly looking to see if there were those who were worthy of my valuable treasures. Would they take care of them? There is a seeming contradiction with trust, though. Trust requires risk. You must choose to trust before you find out if someone is trustworthy. It is possible to start with something small and work up, but ultimately, the only way you find out if someone can be trusted with anything is to give it to them. Yet, I was too concerned with safety to trust. With the exception of sports, I wanted the reward without the risk. On the field or on the court, it was different. Those were probably the only places I really participated in friendship.

I think necessity and natural boundaries are what drove me to function in a healthier, relational way when it came to football. The purpose was clear: become the best football team we could and win every game. There was no ambiguity there. Those who didn't buy into that purpose were left on the outside. If a teammate was in it for himself or simply "for the fun of it," he wasn't trustworthy. If the commitment wasn't there, the relationship wasn't there, and it was easy to see. Of course, we were still on the same team. We were still friendly. But we were not friends (not unless there was something outside of football that drew us together).

However, for those of us who were committed and wanted to win, a bond was created. And to an extent, that bond was irrespective of whether we liked each other. The commitment to each other in that shared purpose formed a relationship that also fostered trust, accountability, and transparency.

If you didn't work out, you would hear about it. If you didn't give it your all or missed an assignment, you were held accountable. When you made a play, you were celebrated. There was sincere joy felt for the success of the other person because his success contributed toward our shared purpose. Their success was my success. And there was trust too. I trusted my teammates to do their job. Because of their commitment, I trusted my teammates to fulfill their responsibility.

But sometimes they didn't. Sometimes I didn't. And sometimes we didn't win. Sometimes there were injuries, loss, and pain. And we grieved together as well.

It was a different relationship than the all-in sharing of life that I was yearning for as a seventeen-year-old. I wasn't sharing my whole life or my whole self with my teammates. I was sharing a specific purpose. It wasn't so much that I was inviting my teammates into line with me as much as I looked around and saw others in the same line, and rather than go it alone as a collection of strangers in line, we struck up a conversation. We helped each other get to the end of this specific line. Our shared commitment allowed me to trust on a relatively shallow level while evaluating whether some of these people could be trusted on a deeper one.

I know this was just sports and only a very short period of my life, but I also know that it was representative of what good friendships really are. The qualities of the relationships that sometimes show up in a locker room or field of play are the same qualities that show up in a business, fieldhouse, barracks, on a board, a neighborhood, or the sidelines of a kid's baseball game because mutual commitment, shared purpose, is a necessary component for friendship.

That commitment allows us the ability to walk in the light, to be transparent in terms of our shared commitment. Of course, because commitment is the key ingredient for friendship, the character of your friend is also of critical importance. A business partner of low character cannot be trusted to honor his commitment. It makes them untrustworthy, which calls their commitment into question. An untrustworthy friend doesn't offer you any comfort (strength *with*) toward the goal. A relationship with these types of people makes you weaker, not stronger.

My senior year in high school, the teachers in my district went on strike. I'm sure this was a long time in coming, but as a student, I wasn't aware of the buildup. I was working my summer job and getting ready for my last year of school. I went to leadership camp with the other ASB officers. I started football two-a-day practices. It was a normal August for me.

Then word came that the teachers were going on strike, and I had two reactions: excitement and anxiety. Of course, the excitement came from the best present my teachers could give me going into my last year of high school – I was now in possession of days and, dare I hope, weeks of work-free, extended summer. My hope was that the administration and union would not be able to get along for at least a few weeks. However, I also had a fair bit of anxiety surrounding whether or not they would cancel the only thing that I couldn't replace. My last year of football was not something that could be put off or rescheduled. As long as they let us play, this was shaping up to the be the best school year ever.

Looking back thirty years later, you may assume that through maturity and experience, I now know that football is just a sport and the value of my education far outweighed the temporary joy of running around on a field with other boys, that the contractual negotiations of our teachers and the struggle for higher pay and better working conditions coinciding with the sacrifices they were willing to make exercising their only point of leverage has changed my perspective on what was truly important during that fall of 1990. You might assume that, but you would be wrong.

Even thirty years ago, sports were one of the last bastions of healthy manhood allowed. Please understand that I am not saying women don't enjoy sports. What women enjoy or dislike is beside the point. The point is that on the field, we were allowed to compete. We were allowed physical confrontation. We were allowed to hold each other accountable and be intolerant of poor efforts. We were allowed to run, yell, fight, celebrate, and mourn. We were allowed to let our actions speak louder than our words. We were not just allowed to do these things. We were encouraged to do them.

This window of opportunity to be guiltlessly male, is incredibly fleeting. For the vast majority of everyone who ever plays them, organized sports last ten years or less. And for those of us whose choice of sport is football, the window is even smaller.

Football is a grown man's sport. You can enjoy and play it when you are younger, but many of the skills and intricacies of the game simply cannot be performed until your body is nearing maturity. So, if you are not a college football player, and over 95 percent of us aren't, you have maybe three or four years to truly experience and enjoy the sport. And because football is such a physical sport, many football players really only play significant time or any time at all during their senior year. You look forward to that year with longing. You covet the opportunity. You greedily hold onto it while you have it, and for nearly everyone who loves the game, it ends in despair.

If you haven't experienced it, you are just going to have to take my word for it. There is a depression that sets in after every high-school football season. Unlike virtually every other sport, almost every senior on the football team knows that he will never play again. Win or lose, by December of your senior year in high school, football is dead.

So, no. My perspective has not changed. If anything, thirty years of life has actually taught me that my seventeen-year-old perspective didn't appreciate the preciousness of my opportunity as much as I should have. It has taught me that the downplaying of the significance of healthy, purposeful relationships that are essentially absent in public schools outside of sports or clubs is usually done by arrogant and bitter human beings with more baggage behind their stance than they want to admit. It doesn't matter, though. In 1990, while the teachers were on strike, they let us play, and it was glorious.

I didn't have a job. I didn't have homework. I could sleep in, watch TV, work out, hang out with friends, and play ball. At seventeen, it literally doesn't get better than that. In fact, at nearly fifty, it still sounds pretty outstanding.

During this short period of pseudo-professional athleticism we enjoyed during the strike, there was little to distract from the goal of playing and winning football games. While the commitment was not the same for everyone on the team, even those who were more casual in their participation simply weren't pulled in other directions. We may have had jobs or other commitments, but without the hours of dictated time that school represented, there was plenty of margin for completing the few responsibilities that most seventeen-year-olds have outside of history and literature. The teachers' strike left us an unusually cohesive unit in our commitment to football and indirectly encouraged time together outside of practice for parties, movies, or just hanging out.

The result was friendship that, for a short time, blossomed out of shared life and purpose. The majority of us would not have spent time together outside of the fact that we were on the same team. To one degree or another, we were all committed to playing football.

Had school been going, that commitment would have necessarily waned as other, differing priorities would have demanded attention. But without school, regardless of where football fell in each person's hierarchy of importance, the removal of eight hours a day of obligated time left room for football to take a larger role in each of our lives. We were committed to the game, and because of that commitment, we developed strong relationships to each other.

We went undefeated. We won every game we played. We played better than we ever had before. But it didn't last. Unfortunately, the teachers' union and school district came to an agreement, and school started again. Daily life went back to the grind of getting up, shuffling from class to class, practice, homework, and sleep. Our focus became diffused.

Studying, SATs, homecoming, ASB, family responsibilities, work, sleep, all of it began vying for our attention. Commitment waned, and relationships became more distant.

We tried to hold on with team parties and get togethers. We were still closer than we likely would have been had we not enjoyed six weeks of uninterrupted time together, but the longer we were back in school, the more we reverted back to the regular pressures of life, the more our individual priorities interfered with our shared commitment.

It didn't all fall apart though. We still won one or two more games, but we definitely didn't play as well. And we lost the last two games of the season (our only losses) and missed going to the state playoffs. But man! It was fun while it lasted.

I have learned since then that my experience in my final year of high school wasn't unique at all. Ok, being an unpaid professional athlete is not something everyone gets to do, but the types of relationships that come and go from a shared commitment or season of life is a regular and natural occurrence. We call these relationships friendships.

Of course, calling someone a friend today is a bit ambiguous. In telling a story, you may say "a friend of mine told me...," but that use of "friend" usually just means someone you know or are "friendly" with. Or, a *friend* can be someone you have fun with but also someone of whom you don't have any significant knowledge. Or, a *friend* may just be someone willing to listen to your stories or looks at your social media posts. A *friend* can also be a somewhat-close relationship. In that case, we may have to call that person a *best friend* to differentiate between the friendships that are relatively shallow and this more authentic or exclusive friendship. However, this may cause some conflict by bestowing the honorific of *best friend* to one friend over another. It might make your other *friends* feel excluded (even if, in reality, they are), so many people, regardless of the necessary grammatical contradiction in meaning, have more than one *best friend* (Man! This is getting complicated). Fortunately, though, messaging vernacular has solved this problem for us, and we have a new category that is slightly better than the lowly *best friend*: the BFF or *best friend forever*. Now that is special! Unless, of course, you have more than one BFF...

It could be that the word "friend" used to carry more significance. I think it is likely that a friend used to be considered a more exclusive thing. Regardless of whether or not the meaning has changed over time, today, a friend is a temporary relationship of varying degrees of seriousness. And like all relationships, friendship is defined by shared commitment, and that commitment leads to some portion of shared life. And shared life, *living with* each other, is the stuff of strength. It offers comfort during the times of pain, and that is how we all make it through life.

If we are going to acquire comfort (the strength that comes from *living with*) in this life, then one of the first rings of relationships that we develop is our community of friends. Again, the key is commitment. Friendships, whether they are initiated by a mutual commitment to your high school football team, your neighborhood, your child's soccer team, or your work spring from a shared commitment. That commitment requires a degree of walking in the light, but really only to the degree of the commitment.

Rarely is this commitment overtly stated or agreed to. It simply exists simultaneously with someone else. Most of the time, we are just going about our lives, elementary school, high school, or work, and we notice that there are others going through the same stage of life as we are. In a sense, we are already sharing life, and some of these people are fun, compatible, or enjoyable to be around.

These are friendships of proximity, and they are often the shallowest and most fleeting of our friendships. They rarely grow beyond someone you talk to during the soccer game or with whom you pass the time during your shift. While they make the time you share more enjoyable and the *waiting in line* more bearable, there is little expectation that these friends will show up during a real time of need because any shared commitment here is of a secondary nature. I may be committed to my child, so I commit to being at the soccer games, but I am not committed to the other parents to any extent other than to the degree that it helps my child. The same goes for school, work, church, or whatever. There is no significant relationship here unless the reason that you are showing up in proximity to each other is because you are both committed to the same thing, like my football team in high school, launching a business, or sitting on an advisory board.

This is where the beginnings of true friendship begin. Truly shared commitment to a cause or an endeavor creates a bond. It creates and requires trust, must be reciprocal, and must be done in the light.

You can't reciprocate a friendship or even experience one in the dark because if the other party doesn't know who you are, he can't be a friend to you. He hasn't even met you. When you hide, pretend, or put on a mask of who you think he may find more attractive, he is engaging in a relationship with someone who doesn't exist. Hiding who you are, what you are, or pretending to be someone you aren't may seem safer, but it ultimately negates the potential for comfort in your life.

This is why walking in light is absolutely essential to share even the smallest part of your life. To share a commitment, he must know you are committed. If it is work, a club, or an exercise class, a necessary element is being honest about your commitment. To share a season of life, he must know you are with him in that season.

"That's my daughter out there with the pigtails playing defender." Faking it just doesn't get you there. You may be able to trick him for a time, but pretending to be someone you are not to acquire a friend defeats the purpose. Pretending you are committed to a cause is flakey at best, and at worst, will be seen as betrayal. Showing up at a soccer game and pretending to be related to one of the players is just creepy. The bottom line is that if the other person spends enough time with you, eventually, he will see who you really are and the discovery of deception will leave you even more alone than you were when you tried to trick him into friendship in the first place.

While the requirement of authenticity is non-negotiable in friendship, authenticity does not have to equate to absolute transparency. I can show someone who I really am without unloading all the skeletons in my closet into the front room. Walking in light is being honest about your likes and dislikes, weaknesses and strengths, passions, fears, and interests. This honesty needs to be proportional and appropriate to the relationship you are fostering, though. I don't need to tell the parent I'm working with at the fundraiser about my medical ailments. You can choose to hold back some things, but non-disclosure and deception are very different.

I walk in the light by being honest about crying at a movie or admitting that I enjoyed *Downton Abbey*. I walk in the light by apologizing for being late without making up convoluted circumstances as to why it happened. I walk in the light by confessing my enjoyment of a song, food, book, speaker, or hobby without the added false narrative designed to hedge against disapproval. Deception is darkness. Honesty is light. And there is no comfort in darkness.

There is nuance to this. Those of us who have dabbled in the light find out quickly that walking in the light and walking in utter transparency are not the same thing. While walking in light is appropriate virtually all of the time, living in a glass house is not. There are things you do in private that the world does not need to see. I invite people into my house and private life, but, for the most part, I have boundaries. It isn't appropriate, but furthermore, it isn't safe to allow the entire world into the depths of my being.

This goes for strangers for sure, but it also applies to friendships. I don't need to bare my soul to my friend. I do not need to unload my struggles with addiction to the parent of my son's basketball teammate. I don't need to confess my issues with earning the love of my parent with my poker buddies. I don't need to confess my infidelity to my colleague at work.

These people all stepped into line with me to a degree: for a season or purpose. But they did not enter in utterly and completely. Walking in the light is critical for engendering and maintaining relationships, but there is a distinction between deceptions and boundaries. Telling someone that you do not have issues is a lie. Being unwilling to discuss them with someone who is not committed to you is still truthful, still walking in light.

A friend may not be someone who is willing to walk through all of life with you. She may not be a person to be there regardless of circumstances. He may not be the one you count on in your old age. But not everyone can fulfill that kind of relationship. Not everyone can provide that depth of comfort.

A friend, then, commits on a lesser level. A friend commits to a season. A friend commits to a circumstance. A friend walks through a soccer season, elementary school, or business venture with you. A friendship is a limited relationship, and as such, over-disclosing runs the risk of casting pearls before swine.

This is why comfort is reciprocal. There must be a balance in disclosure. I can only enter into a relationship with a person to the degree that he willing to enter in. Friendship cannot be a one-way street. Frankly, not everyone is a friend. A person's ability or willingness to commit is the driver of his ability to be a friend to you. A person's honesty, quality of walking in the light determines not only how much is shared with you, but also how much you can share. Said succinctly, character matters.

A business partner not committed to the business is, frankly, not a business partner. A friend deceiving you about himself is not a friend. A parent who doesn't show up to the baseball games does not become your baseball season companion.

Consistency, commitment, honesty... character—at the heart of every relationship is a level of trust. You must be able to trust each other to be who and what you say you are. A flake can never be a close friend.

CHAPTER 9

FAMILY – STRENGTH FOR THE LONG HAUL

EVERY NOW AND then, you run into the kind of friend who is trustworthy on a deeper level, someone willing to disclose and wait in line, not just for a season but for you. These are people that move beyond seasonal comfort. They enter irrespective of seasons. They stick with you through cancer, divorce, addiction, and poverty. And you stick with them too. These people are truly waiting in line with you, not just holding a place. These people get to see more of your house. And when you describe them, using the word friend falls short. They are more than friends. They are more than partners. It seems closer to the truth to call them brother, sister, husband, or wife. These people are lifers. Till death do us part—family.

When I was still in my twenties and my wife was pregnant with our first child, I worked as a high school teacher. One day, during my planning period, I entered the staff room and an older, more experienced teacher asked how I was doing. It seemed one of those small-talk questions that you don't take seriously, so I answered that I was doing well and expected to continue walking to my desk and work on lessons, grading, or whatever the day held for me. But to my surprise, this man continued. He asked me how things were going with my wife, the pregnancy, how I was looking forward to it, and how I was feeling about it.

Honestly, I got a little annoyed but also felt a little guilty about being annoyed. I had work to do. I only had about forty minutes to knock off as much of my tasks as possible before having to be back in class. I recognized that this man was being kind. He was taking interest and didn't have to. I valued his interest, but frankly, I didn't have time for it. My principles won out, though, and I engaged half-heartedly in the conversation since I knew that people and relationships were more important than getting a forty-minute jump on the hours of work a young teacher needs to do each day outside of class.

Twenty years later, I don't remember his name, but I remember his face. I can picture him at his desk as he turned to me and took time from whatever he was working on to engage with an ignorant and self-assured twenty-seven-year-old. I remember his kindness.

I remember one other thing. I remember answering one of his questions with the belief that I was ready for my daughter to be born. I informed him that my wife and I had planned it out, that we had waited several years to have kids. We had married young and wanted children but also knew that it probably wasn't the best idea to add children to a young marriage. We needed time just being married before adding the responsibilities of parenthood. Our allotted time was over, though, and in accordance with the plan, we were now starting our family. We had waited four years, and we were ready, to which he answered, "No, you aren't."

Well, that was mean. Or it was wrong, odd, awkward, or all of the above. I didn't know what it was, but what had happened to that kind man from just a few seconds ago? What do you mean I am not ready? You don't know me. You don't understand how prepared I am for this. You don't know how much I want to be a dad. I am more than ready. But I should give him the benefit of the doubt. This man had really been kind. He probably didn't mean it that way. He just didn't know the context.

So, I explained that I really was ready. We were both ready. We'd discussed this, read books (ok, I read part of one book, but Kari read books), and had looked forward to it. I was as ready as I could be. I was ready!

"No. You aren't."

Ok, maybe he wasn't kind. Maybe he was just a lovable moron. He probably saw the utter confusion on my face, so he continued, "You can't be ready. It's impossible. In a couple of months, your life is going to change."

"I know," I interrupted.

"No, you don't. You can't know. The second your child is born, the very instant it happens, everything changes. It will hit you like a sledgehammer."

"I know."

"No. You don't. Absolutely everything changes, your marriage, identity, everything; the way you drive, the way you watch movies, the reason you go to work and the reason you leave work. As soon as your child is born, you are a dad. And nothing is ever the same."

Thanks, Gandalf. I'm just going to walk over here now and grade one-third of an essay with the eight minutes I have left in my planning period. Ok?

I should have called him Moses, because just like the prophecies of old, a couple of months later, that conversation came rushing back to me like a sledgehammer to the chest. Our daughter was born, and we were leaving the hospital. Kari and I were absolutely thrilled with our beautiful baby girl. It makes me cry thinking about it even today. She was perfect. We held her and each other. We talked to her, fed her, and changed her. That day or so in the hospital was a really sweet time.

Then it was time to go home. I went and retrieved the car while they wheeled Kari down to the entrance of the hospital. They checked that I had the car seat installed correctly. I grabbed my baby, who was wedged in her little carrier like a crystal vase ready for cross-country shipping. I helped Kari into the car, walked around the other side, stepped behind the wheel, and just about soiled myself.

What the hell was going on?! These people were professionals. They knew about this stuff. And they had just put a one-day-old child in the car with me and said, "Good luck, dude." What were they thinking?! I didn't know anything about taking care of a baby. I had never done this before. They literally just handed me the most fragile and precious thing on this earth, and I strapped it into a metal projectile of death. And they were smiling!

Holy %$@#! I am so not ready for this! And... Bam! Cue the Peter Gabriel music: Sledgehammer. I think I drove an average of twenty-four miles per hour on the way home.

What dawned on me in the days, months, and years to come is that before my daughter, I wasn't a dad. I couldn't be a dad. I didn't have a child. I don't mean to say that you can't be a father without biologically producing a child. That isn't the point. There are other ways to become a father. What I'm saying is that until you have a child, you aren't a parent. It is an absolute. There is a single criteria for parenthood: children. You cannot be one without them.

The scary part of what I learned is that the inverse is not true. Once you have a child, you are a parent, but once you are a dad, you can't un-become one. The change is permanent.

At some point later, the truth of this stared me in the face and turned my blood cold. For the rest of my life, I am a dad. Regardless of whether I leave my wife or abandon my child, I am a dad. From this point forward, I only have power over the modifier. I can be a good or bad dad. I can be an abusive, neglectful, absentee, or deadbeat dad. Or I can be a loving, encouraging, wise, or strong dad.

I no longer had any control over the dad part, and neither did my daughter. I knew that at some point down the road, I might really screw up. I might hurt her in a way that would cause her to say that I was no longer her father. She might shut me out. She might rescind that title. She might move away and never talk to me again.

I looked into that potential future and was chilled to realize that if that were to happen, I would be on the other side, alone and ashamed, knowing that I was still her dad, whether she recognized it or not. And I vowed to myself to do everything in my power to avoid that potential future. Even though I knew that I was flawed, could screw up, fail in one way or many ways over the years, even though I knew it was beyond my ability, if I was now a dad, I was committed to being the best dad I could be.

There is a commitment that goes along with being in a family that continues far beyond the commitment of a friendship. It extends beyond circumstance and seasons. It extends beyond liking the person.

I don't always like the members of my family, but that doesn't end the relationship. If I don't like a friend, he stops being a friend. If I don't like my brother, he passes me the turkey at Thanksgiving (I like my brother. Gary, this is just an example. I'm not trying to send you a message buried in a book).

There is an abundance of movies, books, and TV shows about the difficulty of getting together with family you don't like. This is a fact of life: Anyone you spend years with will annoy you. And, brace for it, you will annoy them too. Your family knows you. They know your quirks and idiosyncrasies. They know your bad habits and flaws. They know how to push your buttons. They know how to make you laugh. They share your stories. And oddly, much of the laughter and joy of getting together with family is commiserating over the shared pain in your lives. Stories that make outsiders cringe reinforce the bond between family members.

That is the purpose of family. Rather than a partner for a season, a companion to share the good times, or the friend that is specifically joining with you for something good or successful, when the storms come, disaster strikes, or pain blots out the good in this life, family members put a hand on your shoulder and remind you that this is why they are there. You can go to the party with your friend, but if you get in a car accident on the way home, your family is who shows up.

This creates such a strange tension as a parent. Here are these beautiful children you share life with, nurture, and guide, and as they near adulthood, assuming a good relationship with your son or daughter, you begin to like them. In many ways, they share the characteristics of the people you seek out as friends. They share the same seasons with you. They have similar or compatible interests. They remind you of yourself, spouse, or both.

But your child is not your friend. The relationship is different. They are family, and as a dad, I am specifically here for the pain. I am here for the hard times. I want to be there for the good times. I want to go to the party and play catch. I want to talk, hike, and travel with my children, but whenever there is a choice between the fun of friendship and the commitment of family, I choose family, knowing that the choice may likely cause more pain and risks my ability to participate in the friendship.

The commitment of family, the commitment to be comfort for the bad times is too important to neglect. This is the comfort that allows us to withstand the pain that is an ever-present aspect of this world. This is the strength necessary for navigating life. And this is why marriage is such a beautiful, powerful, and fragile thing.

Marriage is the act of choosing family. You aren't born into it. You opt into it. You meet someone. You spend time with them. You love them. You commit to them. Then you choose over and over again to spend time with them. And you choose to continue to love them, even when the friendship fades.

There aren't always good times in marriage. In fact, everyone knows there are bad times. You intentionally sign up for the bad times. Kari and I, like many people, specifically called this out in our wedding vows:

"I, Joel, take you, Kari to be my wife, to have and to hold from this day forward, for better, for worse, for richer, for poorer, in sickness and in health, to love and to cherish, until death do us part."

I promised to spend my life being there for her, no matter what. My hope on that day was a marriage filled with joy and passion. But my promise was to hold, love, and cherish her during the pain. My promise was to be more than her friend. I was promising to be her husband. I opted into her family.

I believe this is also why divorce is so destructive. Divorce divides family. Divorce undermines the strength necessary for life. And just like a deadbeat dad, that relationship can change, but it doesn't truly end. Family members may become estranged, and they may betray their commitment, but family never really stops being family. From that point forward, I'm just a good, a bad, or an ex-husband.

As I'm writing this book, I've been married for twenty-five years. I love my wife dearly. She is beautiful, intelligent, and caring. She is faithful to her word and to me. And yes, she drives me crazy. Because I would like to reach year twenty-six, I won't list the things that infuriate me about her. Let's just say that there are many ways in which she goes about her daily life that, in moments of stress or fatigue, make me want to kick things (you know, slippers I may trip on walking to the bathroom, a curling iron left on my side of the counter, another box of tea in the cupboard, the third jar of pickles in the fridge, an aluminum can with just a swallow or two left in the bottom, hair in the drain...), but it wouldn't be fair or smart to list things in a book like this.

This is not fair because Kari doesn't have a voice here. This is not smart because I have it on good authority (my wife) that I drive her nuts too. I am insensitive and self-absorbed. I procrastinate. I say really stupid things. And I have absolutely no concept of time; on time, late, early, days, hours, minutes? It is like a foreign language to me. I push Kari's buttons like no one else in her life. But she is there for me. She is my wife. She is comfort and safety. Usually... And I am there for her. I am constant and faithful and supportive. Most of the time...

The first time I saw pornography, I was thirteen or fourteen years old. Nowadays, that's pretty old to be exposed, but I think it was pretty normal then. There was no internet or smart phones in the 1980s that allowed pre-teens unfettered access to the human trafficking industry. Back then, pornography was almost solely limited to magazines and videos you could only find in dirty, dimly lit buildings in the bad part of town.

What you found in those stores, though, was the kind of pornography that debases people to the point of repulsive perversion. It removes all intimacy and love from the sex act and reduces and transforms it into a graphic portrayal of biological functions and animalistic lust depicted through close-ups of body parts and acts of abuse, but no one starts there.

Middle school boys didn't generally have access to that kind of thing. For us, we needed to sneak into R-rated movies or sneak peaks at magazines on the top shelf of the bookstore magazine display. To ogle naked women in the 80s, I just needed to be a little uncomfortable and take a risk of getting caught in some kind of public forum—which was still a fairly good deterrent for a middle schooler.

The pornography that I was exposed to was seemingly more innocent than the back-alley variety, but to categorize pornography only by the hardcore versions that are evoked by the word is like limiting the category of drugs to only heroine or crack cocaine. Very few people begin their foray into drug abuse by shooting up heroine. Heroine is where you end up when you want it bad enough to debase yourself in those dirty, dimly lit buildings in the bad part of town next to the adult bookstore.

No, I didn't start with an XXX movie. You don't do that. You start with glimpses of breasts in 80s movies that included women who, for no particular reason other than that it is seemingly how the alternate reality of Hollywood in the 80s worked, seemed to always want to take off their tops either before getting killed or the result of a joke (funny thing is that no matter how funny or scary the movie, I was never laughing or scared during those scenes). You started with those movies. You started with something seemingly more innocuous, something that still pretends to honor the delicate beauty of women, something that despite this pretending, is more insidious, something that objectifies, but in a soft light that allows you to believe it honors beauty rather than stripping away the life that allows beauty to exist. In the 1980s, you started with secretive issues of Playboy magazine.

For me, it was the Vanna White issue. I admit this for two reasons: First, I know that anyone who grew up in the 80's knows who she is and the allure for an adolescent boy that she was. Second, whether it was done legally or not, the publication of revealing pictures of someone against their will is truly repulsive. I don't know the legal subtleties around publishing, nor am I commenting on them, but virtually everyone agrees on the applicable standard of conduct. That is, just because you can do a thing doesn't mean you should. And any decent person understands that to take a picture of someone, even of a consenting person, and then to show other people against the express wishes of the subject of the picture is a violation of basic decency. A moderately moral person wouldn't do it, even if the only complaint was "My hair looks terrible!" But here, publishers hide behind their legal rights in violation to their moral duty to another human.

This is the core of the problem with pornography, even the seemingly innocuous kinds like gratuitous nude scenes in movies or Playboy magazines. Pornography exploits the freedom we enjoy while ignoring the dignity, value, and preciousness of individual human life. Pornography distances the individual from the act. Pornography separates the body from the person. Pornography removes the risk of human vulnerability from the most intimate of human interactions. Aah! And there is the draw.

Why is shared life so elusive? Because sharing your life, sharing yourself, is immensely risky, and rejection of that invitation to share is actual rejection of who I am at my core. And nothing hurts more than that. So, the fantasy realm of pornography allows us to pretend that someone wants us without having to share anything. It reduces a necessarily reciprocal relationship to a directional one and additionally removes even the risk from that directional transaction by making it 100 percent successful; no risk of rejection, no need to walk in light, and no comfort.

Beyond the abject depravity of pornography is a greater problem though. While we indulge in the unreality or fantasy, the seemingly risk-free transaction of fictitiously fulfilled desire, we simultaneously exist in the real world with real people with whom we have real relationships. And in the real world, light eventually finds the darkness.

For me, my wife eventually discovered my struggles with pornography. Frankly, I don't remember how or when, but she found out. And it was really embarrassing. I was ashamed. But it also felt good that it had come to light. It felt good to bring my struggles into the open so they could finally be dealt with. . . until later when you're found out again, and then again.

Don't misunderstand here. This section is not about pornography. It is about the betrayal of trust. Regardless of the shame I felt, the power I allowed pornography to have over me, or the perversion that pornography is, the subject of this story is Kari.

I shared my life with my wife, but she shared hers with me as well. I committed to her. I made vows. I told her I would be there for her, no matter what, as long as I drew breath. I would wait in line with her for the long haul. And I was. I was in line with her.

And several hours into waiting in line together, she realized that sometimes while I was standing beside her,

I was imagining that I was in line with someone else. It doesn't matter that I didn't physically step out of line. How could she take that any other way than I was not really in line with her at all? How could she interpret my struggles with pornography as anything else than a rejection of her value? How could she see my shameful dalliances with images of women as anything other than an example of what I would do if there was no risk associated with it? And she was right. You know she was right. You know that is exactly what pornography is. It is the avenue for which our free will travels when the consequences of our actions are removed. And that is when Kari began to realize that I was human. And humans cannot be trusted.

That's the problem. We need comfort to navigate this life. We need people. But despite the best intentions, strongest integrity, and the firmest commitment, people always fail. Friends fail. Family members fail. Husbands fail. Wives fail.

Years later, Kari and I are still together. She has forgiven me... many times for many things. Along the way, I have forgiven her too as I realized her humanity as well. We are still committed to each other. We are still together. And we are closer than we were when we were first married and living under the illusion of love conquering all (maybe it does, but my ability to love absolutely does not).

The problem is that the strength of my commitment to my wife is limited by the depth of my character. I can only commit to the extent that my integrity keeps me from betraying that commitment, which is also the good news. As I have grown, I have matured. As I have matured, my character has deepened. Through trials, pain, and challenge, with the help of the comfort of my wife, parents, siblings, and friends, I have become stronger. And that allows me more strength to lend to Kari, to all of them.

But I am still flawed. I always will be. There is no pinnacle of human existence. There is only the climb. The further you travel, the further you realize you still have to go. Human perfection is the delusion of an ignorant mind. Improvement? Yes. Perfection? Not a chance.

So, I am a better husband, father, brother, son, and friend than I was years ago, and I plan on being better yet in the future, but both Kari and I have learned that while I am family for her, while I am a closer and more committed kind of family than even the other family members, I will fail her, and she will fail me. My father will fail me. My son will fail me, and my friends, business partners, and family members will. We are all human. We are all flawed. And we all fail.

Chapter 10

Immanuel – Strength Now and Forever

THE BLESSING AND curse of youth is the ignorance of our limitations. When I was young, my aspirations were almost limitless. I believed I could do and be anything. I was smart, strong, fast, funny, a leader, a good person, and a hard worker. I was going to be president of the United States someday. I was going to be a Supreme Court justice. I was going to be a professional football player. For a brief time, I even imagined myself becoming a super hero. Whatever I wanted was in reach. If I set my mind to it, I could do it.

This vision of unlimited potential and endless possibility leads young people to develop, innovate, and bless the world with giant leaps forward in thinking and advancement. While there are always exceptions, in general, old people don't innovate. Invention and

boundary-pushing is the purview of the young, especially because they don't see the boundaries or at least
don't agree that the boundaries should exist.

The young have a unique ability to think outside the
box in part because they simply haven't built the box yet.
This is a wonderful aspect of youth. It is valuable. It is
necessary for our world, community, and culture. The
old must be reminded by the young of the achievement
that is possible through the existence of belief and hope.

As the stories on which I grew up of Roger Banister
and World War II soldiers illustrate, many of the limitations we place on ourselves are of our own invention. The
blessing and curse of youth is being unaware of those
limitations; the blessing from the achievement, inno-
vation, and hope that comes from a life lived without
perceived limitation; the curse from the inevitable point
that reality disabuses us of this fantasy.

When I was in my early 30s, I worked as portfolio
manager in an investment advisory firm, and I was
able to participate in a due diligence trip for hedge
fund managers. It was a great trip. I loved it; meetings in Manhattan, dining in restaurants, and learning
from some of the best financial minds in the world. It
remains one of the best business trips of my life. It was
also the source of a pivot in my understanding of my
place in the world.

One of the meetings took place in Greenwich,
Connecticut. We drove up and sat across from a partner

of a large and very successful hedge fund. I don't recall his name or education, but I do remember him as being very intelligent, and knowledgeable, and articulate in his ability to explain and sell incredibly complex financial premises, principles, and the applications of those premises and principles within their fund. This guy was a top-one-percenter for sure—smarter than most of the people I had ever come into contact with. And I felt like I belonged. I was following him. I understood him, not just the words he was saying, but the concepts he was explaining. I may not have had the industry experience that he had, but there was nothing he was saying that was beyond or above me.

It was really quite a boost to my ego. I had always been smart. I had good grades but didn't need to try that hard to get them. I could argue, process, and conclude better than most of the people I had met. There really wasn't a subject in school that I struggled with. Through all my vast experience, I found that I was among the smartest people in the world (forgive me. I was young).

As I've said, I grew up with my dad emphasizing the story of Roger Banister. And while I latched onto the part of the story that implies you can do anything you put your mind to, that really isn't what my dad was trying to emphasize. Dad would say that the tale of the four-minute mile is not an inherently encouraging story of unlimited potential but a cautionary tale of being careful not to accept limitations that are not really there.

There is a subtle difference there. The first implies no limitations. The second implies that limitations exist but may be much less restrictive than we assume. And Dad would follow up at other times with the axiom that we needed to work hard because there will always be someone else out there that is bigger, faster, stronger, or smarter than you are. Taken as a whole, the lesson was this: Don't rest on your laurels. You need to work hard. And through work and sacrifice, you can achieve greater things than you may have believed possible and, furthermore, exceed the accomplishments of more gifted people who limit themselves because of their perception of limitations or lack of grit.

So, as I made my way to Manhattan that autumn, there was a bit of nervousness attached to the trip. While I had long since been disabused of my superiority on the bigger, faster, stronger spectrum, I had never to that point met anyone who had made me feel limited in my intellect. But I knew that stepping into the world of 2004 New York City hedge fund management was stepping into the world of some of the smartest people on the planet.

And here I was, sitting across from one of them, holding my own. I truly was feeling pretty pleased with how I stacked up against one of the best minds in the world. Sure, he had knowledge that I simply didn't have. And I would never have argued that I was somehow above him or could replace the years of expertise and success that he had, but it was also clear to me that had life gone differently, and I had found myself in similar circumstances to him, I had no doubt that I could perform at his level (or above, considering my exceptional grit).

However, as I sat there chatting after the presentation, enjoying the self-satisfied glow of my confirmed genius, he said something that ruined it all. He said, "I'm the moron around here. My job is to talk to the regular people because the smart guys are impossible to understand." And then he proceeded to give us a tour around the building, introducing us to analysts, programmers, and strategists that left me feeling like a border collie in a calculus lecture. *Hey man, don't get down on yourself. Border collies are really smart dogs!* That was when I learned the breadth of the gap between me and the truly smart people in the world. No amount of my inflated sense of grit or denial of limitations would allow my butt sniffing, treat-loving, sheep-herding self to grasp what these people understood. I simply wasn't on their level. I was limited.

The blessing and curse of youth is the ignorance of our limitations. The blessing and curse of age is the knowledge of those limitations. The older I get, the more I understand the inescapable reality of my inevitable failure. I'm simply a flawed individual. I soften that blow with relative comparisons. We all do. I'm better than most. I'm not as bad as many. I'm relatively honest. It helps our self-esteem. It bolsters our self-worth.

You don't use these relative qualifiers after you've won the world championships. After Usain Bolt set the world record in the hundred-meter and was called the fastest man in the world, he didn't qualify it by saying he was faster than most or pointing out that he wasn't as fast as a cheetah. You qualify your status because you recognize your limitations.

"I'm relatively honest" is what liars say. I say that because I know I'm a liar but don't want to accept that negative label. And, heck, I don't lie as much as that other guy! But isn't that kind of like saying, "I'm a murderer, sure, but I'm not a serial killer!"?

The reality of our existence is that we are all flawed. I will fail my wife. I have already failed my wife on multiple occasions. I don't want to get out of line with her. I love her. I'm committed to her, but sometimes I find myself at the hotdog stand wondering when I left the line.

And sometimes, my wife finds herself in the same position, whether out of fatigue, boredom, self-absorption, or annoyance, she fails to be there. Kari has flat-out failed me at times, so has my brother, sister, mother, and father. Don't get me wrong. I have a great family. They are better than most... But the problem with my family is that they are made up of humans. Regardless of their commitment, they are all flawed. Regardless of their intentions, they will inevitably fail me.

I understand the temporary nature of my friend-ships. My high school friends never committed to standing with me for life. We went to school together. We played football together. We went our separate ways. It was never supposed to last longer than that, and I don't feel any bitterness that the friend I worked with in my first job out of college isn't in my life anymore. That wasn't the deal.

My wife, though, she committed to being there with me till I died. My dad—my dad will always be my dad. But who doesn't have issues that are directly sourced from how their parents failed them? When a family member fails you, it is a betrayal of trust. It hurts at your core. It is a reminder of the razor-thin division between our existence bolstered by comfort and a life facing pain in the weakness of isolation. When a family member steps away, you feel alone. It reminds you that your best chance in this life hinges on the length of time between the inevitable failures of flawed individuals.

What is the alternative, though? We know that to be alive in this world is to be exposed to pain. We will be hurt. We will experience physical and emotional distress. And we know it is necessary. We know that life simply can't be lived without pain, and we cannot increase our capacity for withstanding pain without experiencing it. We also know that this pain is ultimately more than we can bear. It is bigger than our ability to withstand on our own, and the only remedy for this inescapable and necessary pain is the strength found in relationships—the power of "with." Comfort only comes from living "with" others, and to facilitate those relationships so we can access the strength that allows us to withstand the pain of our lives, we have to step into the light. Yet, stepping into the light, bearing your true self to another exposes you. The light makes you vulnerable to more pain, but the choice is either to hide from the risk of relational letdown or accept the inevitable death that comes from a solitary fight. So, we choose relationships. We access friends to get us through seasons of life. We lean on family to be there, no matter what.

And this works most of the time. Most of the time, if we have had the courage to walk in light and allow others to know and comfort us, we find that we can bear the difficulties of life. We even find that life can be full of joy and pleasure. We hold onto life as a precious, fleeting gift just as we grasp the hands of our family members for as long as we can keep them with us.

But ultimately and intermittently, we find ourselves alone and afraid. We recognize that the relative strength of our "relatives" will fail. And in those quiet times of life, we stare up at the ceiling in the middle of the night trying to shut out the fear, anxiety, or doubt that threatens to cripple us in our daily lives. What then? What are we to do?

If there was no God, sentience would be the cruelest aspect of evolution. Self-awareness in a godless universe is simply waking up to the eventuality of our doom. I would rather be the border collie, seeking affection and sniffing butts until the time it all ends. I wouldn't see it coming. I wouldn't anticipate the pain of rejection, old age, or loss. I would still feel them, sure, but not the anticipation, not the awareness.

The existence of God leaves us with troubling questions as well, though. Why would he create us only to leave us in this state of struggle? Why create us only to let us experience this pain where the only reliable strategy for dealing with it is the comfort of others, yet in a seemingly cruel manipulation provides only flawed and ultimately unreliable people on which to count? Why would he do that?

He didn't.

I have a very commonplace memory from when I was four or five years old. I was in a supermarket with my mom. I'm pretty sure it was K-Mart because I can still picture the blue light on the pole in the middle of the aisle. I was with my mom, and she was shopping while I was looking at Hot Wheels. For those of you too young to know what those are, this harkens back to the days when the objects of play used to have mass. They were manufactured and distributed, not pixelated and stored in the cloud to be interacted with through a controller and a screen. Shortly after the dinosaurs became extinct, little boys and girls would play with small toy cars, and the chief brand among them was Hot Wheels.

I was looking at some Hot Wheels with my mom, because I'm sure that's what we were in K-Mart to do, and I found a beautiful little TransAm. I'm not sure why I liked those so much, but it was beautiful, and just like everyone else that sees something so awe inspiringly beautiful that it takes your breath away as you contemplate the transcendant magnificence capable in our universe, I wanted to share it with someone I loved. My mom needed to see this little toy car! So, I reached over and tugged on her dress. I grabbed the car off the rack and held it up while raising my eyes to make sure I caught the emotion of her first time witnessing toy-car perfection. Only, that wasn't what I saw. Instead, what I saw chilled my bones.

As I looked up, what stared down at me was the most hideous of all creatures in a five-year-old's existence. Staring back at me with a somewhat amused grin on her face was not the adoring face of a mother overcome with joy at the treasure I had unearthed on the racks of the local K-Mart. No, what stared back at me was the most terrifying abomination of civilized society, the betrayal of all that was good in the world. Looking down on me was... a stranger!

This wasn't my mother. Some sicko had sidled up to me, impersonating the source of safety and comfort in my life. It was shocking. Quickly following my shock at the depravity of some people who would counterfeit their place in the most sacred of relationships was the cold realization of betrayal. My mother had left me as prey in the aisles of a superstore. She had abandoned me while I was being seduced by die-cast works of art. She had left me as if I meant nothing to her. Despite the knowledge of her betrayal, there was only one avenue back to safety. I had to search the vast expanse of aisle 23 and reunite with the woman formerly known as Mom.

I whipped my head around, scanning first one way and then the other. There she was, calmly looking at something as mundane as notebook paper or the like, completely oblivious to the danger she had subjected me. There she was—not the counterfeit version, but the real source of strength and safety in my life. Anger, fear, and feelings of betrayal aside, I ran to her. Like some Olympic sprinter, I crossed those fifteen feet like it was no more than five yards, and wrapping my arms around her right leg, I buried my face into the folds of her dress as I tried to shut out the horror of the past few hours (or seconds…).

And that's what happened. At least that is how I remember it.

Throughout my life, I would have the fact that my mom loved me reinforced over and over again. She would never intentionally betray or hurt me, but intentional or not, she let me down. She walked away from me. She abandoned me. As I grew, I learned that the measure of a faithful person is not whether or not this happens, but how often it happens and how much remorse they feel as a result.

I'm not throwing my family under the bus here. I am incredibly fortunate to have the family I have. My parents are still together. My brother and sister live within an hour's drive. My wife loves and puts up with me. But literally everyone I love has let me down at some point. And that isn't unique. Everyone, not just me, has been let down by someone that loves them. We are all human. We are all fallible. It is inevitable.

However, while my mom has blown it at times, it really isn't fair to lay my childhood, K-Mart trauma at her feet. As an adult, I can look back at the story with a bit more perspective. I'm a parent and an adult now and, as such, I can attest to a few things that are beyond a shadow of a doubt.

First, regardless of my perception at the time, we were not at K-Mart to look at Hot Wheels. My mother may have promised that I could look in order to avoid a tantrum, or she may have conceded while we were in the aisle, but she definitely did not pack up the station wagon, make sure I was dressed and ready to go, and drive twenty minutes so I could lust after a two-inch, die-cast TransAm. Regardless of my desire or limited perspective, it wasn't about me.

Second, I was never in danger. Funny thing, danger. Danger is kind of an absolute concept. It isn't really defined by perception. It is defined by truth. Crossing the street blindfolded may or may not be dangerous. Whether or not actual danger exists is completely dependent upon whether or not there are cars or hazards that may cause me harm. Crossing the street blindfolded may be a dangerous activity, but that is based on a probability that, should you repeat the behavior, inevitably, those hazards will present themselves, and the danger will be realized.

Fear, on the other hand, is completely relative and may or may not be connected with the existence of danger at all. I may experience fear because someone blindfolds me and pushes me into the street, only to find out later that they had closed the road, and there was no possibility of being hit by a car. Or I may unknowingly walk into the street while talking with a friend and put my life in real danger with no fear whatsoever.

I was never in danger in K-Mart. My mom was fifteen feet away. She knew where I was and what I was doing. The danger wasn't real, but I was afraid, and that was real. And not only was the fear real, the pain that goes along with the fear, anxiety, and feelings of betrayal; those were real too. I actually experienced those. And the pain of that moment, fortunately, caused me to change my behavior. I really didn't like the feeling of looking up into a stranger's eyes. I did not like the feeling of being alone in the aisle. So for the rest of that trip, I stayed a little closer to my mom. I didn't risk it anymore.

Third, my mother didn't abandon me. She didn't leave me in the aisle on my own, and not even as a relative measure. She didn't walk away from me. I walked away from her.

I saw something I wanted. I saw something that I thought would bring me pleasure or simulate comfort, and I walked across the aisle to be closer to the object of my desire. I didn't intend to leave my mother. I just got distracted. The TransAm caught my eye, and I wandered away.[17]

Last, it took me looking away from what had caught my eye and becoming aware of my surroundings to realize that I was not at her side anymore. If she had come over and placed her hand on me in the midst of my die-cast infatuation, I would have never realized my separation. I needed to discover that for myself.[18]

The problem arose from my five-year-old perspective. When you are five, you think the world revolves around you. No one's pain is like the pain you experience. There is nothing worse than having what you want withheld from you. You are unaware of other people's perspective. Only yours exists. So, when I looked up and perceived my mother an unaccountably dangerous distance away from me, I could only attribute it to her neglect. But, I say again, I was the one who walked away.

The pain I was experiencing was not due to a danger she had exposed me to but a fear I had inflicted upon myself. There would be no danger or fear if I had stayed at her side.

Whether or not you believe in God doesn't change the fact that you have a relationship with him. A father is a father, whether or not the child recognizes it. It may be a good, bad, or estranged relationship. Where two people exist, and one loves the other, there is a relationship. And that relationship is impacted by the same four truths that I now know about my trip to K-Mart..

God has never left us or exposed us to danger. We have left him. We have chased shiny objects. We have searched after simulated comfort and have been distracted by the wants and desires of our lives. We walk through life, thinking the pain of the moment is monumental and more than we can bear, and we fear the unknown and potential danger around the corner. We view the universe and eternity as if our little aisle in K-Mart is the whole of existence, justice, and meaning. And we feel alone and abandoned. But he is only fifteen feet away. God's love is not distant. We are.

He is waiting in the aisle for me to recognize that I have wandered. He desires to have a relationship with me, a real relationship with the real me, not the facade I put on to impress, not the mask, not the person I pretend to be. He asks me to walk in the light because he already knows what I hide in the darkness. He calls me his son because he is more than a friend. He is family. He is my father.

He knows that the pain is real, even if the danger is not. So, he is also the God of comfort. He is the God of strength from being with. He is the God who solved our struggle, not by telling us to come back to him or telling us to work harder, be better, or be stronger but by providing his son as a way of reuniting and repairing our relationship. While we struggle in the darkness, he shines a light into our pain. So, he named that son Immanuel, which means "God with us."[19] God comforts.

And this is the only reliable solution to our pain. We cannot tough it out on our own. We can try. We can get stronger. We can overcome. We can pick up the Tetris pieces of our lives and try to hold them together, but we will eventually fail. We simply aren't strong enough on our own. We need help.

We need other people and the comfort they provide. We need our seasonal friends, the joy and partnership they provide in our lives, even though we know that it is temporary. We need our family too, the ones who will be with us throughout our lives, no matter what. But we know they will fail. They will get distracted, walk away, or simply die.

In addition to all the things that we need, we need God. He is the only permanent, constant, and faithful presence in our lives in whom we can hope and trust with absolute security. He is the only source of comfort that will not waver. He is the only one who knows all of who we are, whether or not we have brought it into the light, and despite the ugliness that we try to keep hidden, he says, "Absolutely! I'd love to wait in line with you." So he does, and unlike everyone else, he promises that he will never leave or forsake me.

He knows me. He loves me. And he won't step out of line. Ever.

CHAPTER 11

SO, WHAT?!

MY DAD USED to say, "If you are not part of the solution, you are part of the problem." It wasn't a saying he invented, and it wasn't something he said a lot. But it stuck with me.

If I'm not part of the solution, I'm part of the problem. *Man! That's hard.* And it was hard, but this saying has forced me to evaluate the value of pointing out issues. It has forced me to question the validity of naming problems without offering or contemplating solutions. It has forced me to address problems with solutions that included my own actions rather than proposing solutions that only require other people changing their behavior. And it challenged me to evaluate whether or not a problem was truly a problem.

Life is full of pain. Problem? I don't think so. The existence of pain is not something that can be eliminated, nor should it. We don't want to live in a world without pain. We like exertion, spicy foods, and dramatic movies. We actually like manageable pain with positive outcomes. Also, we need growth, and growth doesn't exist without pain. Most importantly, though, unless we eliminate danger, pain is necessary as a warning system. We wouldn't survive without pain.

Pain isn't a problem. Coping with pain, though, that's a problem. Pain is prevalent, inescapable, and necessary. It is also potentially harmful and debilitating. So, the problem question is, "How do you navigate a world where there is an unavoidable and potentially harmful and debilitating or even deadly presence that you must interact with if you wish to live a healthy and full life?"

It's not enough just to call it out. It is not beneficial to only acknowledge that this problem exists. We need to know what to do about it. The problem is coping with pain. The solution is comfort. We need the strength of living with others to deal with the pain of this world, and that solution is only as good as the reliability and constancy of the person with whom you share life. But just calling out the solution is not enough. If you aren't part of the solution, you are part of the problem. The natural question then, is "So, what?!" How do you do it?

It took me about six months in college to realize I had spent most of my life pointed in the wrong career direction. I had always thought I wanted to go into politics. I was active in ASB in school. I took a couple of elective classes in law. I took five years of Russian and even spent a month in the Soviet Union my sophomore year in high school. I had it all mapped out.

Then I went to college, and I couldn't stand it. I still enjoyed politics. I still wanted to address the issues, but I learned very quickly that to get to where I eventually wanted to be, I'd have to wade through years of what I wasn't willing to do.

So, during my second year of college, I found myself floundering, not knowing what I wanted to do, but knowing that I didn't want to do what I had come there to accomplish. With the future trajectory that I had planned no longer the target at which I wanted to shoot, I shifted my focus to the present. Rather than working toward a future goal, I decided to explore what I enjoyed in the moment, even if I couldn't see where it led. So, I went back to my high school and joined the football coaching staff.

It turned out that I loved it. I loved football. I loved teaching. I loved making a difference in the lives of young men, whether for the short or the long term. I loved the strategy and planning. It was all good.

That decision turned into a decision to pursue teaching as a career, which led to counseling, which led to, believe it or not, financial advising, which lead to several other twists and turns in my life. But through it all has been a thread: teaching, coaching, and guiding. Over the past thirty years, I have coached football, basketball, soccer, and baseball. I have taught high school, Sunday school, seminars, and workshops. I have led Young Life groups, church youth groups, men's groups, and discussion groups. I have served on a school board and church board. Oh, and I have been a parent. In short, I have consistently looked for avenues to teach, coach, and guide because that is what I enjoy. That is what I am good at.

Through it all, while I have been trying to help others learn and grow, they have helped me learn and grow. They taught me as I taught them, and among many others, I learned four lessons that inform the "So, what?!"

Lesson 1: The big rocks go in first.

This one comes from a book written by Stephen Covey called *First Things First*[5]. I have never read the book, and when I first heard the story, I didn't even know the source. The lesson is what is important here. I won't tell the story in its entirety as many people have heard it. Suffice to say, you can read his book or search the internet for the story, and you will find it, but it goes like this:

---

[5]   Covey, Stephen R, A. Roger Merrill, and Rebecca R Merrill. *First Things First: To Live, to Love, to Learn, to Leave a Legacy.* New York: Simon & Schuster, 1995.

There is a presenter speaking to some ambitious and upwardly mobile people, and this speaker pulls out a large mason jar and loads it up with large rocks. He then asks the audience if the jar is full, to which they respond, "Yes." He then proves them wrong by pouring some gravel in and asking again. He repeats this pattern with sand and water and then asks the group to discern the lesson. Someone in the group understandably concludes that you can always fit more in, but the speaker corrects the class by saying, "If you don't put the big rocks in first, you'll never get them in at all."

The natural thing for us to do with relationships is to start with the easy ones. Friendships of proximity or circumstance happen organically. Most of us don't have to work that hard to develop at least a few of these. We show up at work, our kid's ballet recital, or first period in high school. We make friends. Some of these friends you have to intentionally pursue, and they become something more. Family relationships, committed partners, spouses... Maintaining these relationships takes work. At some point, these people hurt, anger, or annoy us, and we have to work through it if we want to keep the relationship. And God! He's the toughest! Praying, reading the Bible, going to church or groups—sometimes this one feels completely one-sided.

Here's the deal, if you don't put the big rocks in first, they will never fit. Your jar will become full of the sand of easy friendship, and while your life will feel full and you will feel safe, comforted, and strong during the good times, the storms[20] will inevitably come. Life will knock your jar over and the things that easily pour into your life also easily pour out. If you are full of sand before the storm, you will soon be empty in its midst.

So, big rocks first. You must make time for God every day. Pray. Read. Sing. Meditate. Whatever works for you. Whatever gets you engaging in the relationship that will never fail. Do some of it. Do all of it, but do it. And I promise you, the more you do it, the less one-sided it will become.

Then, family. It is not enough to simply ask God for a good day and then head off to work, come home, eat, watch some TV, and collapse into bed. Did you connect with your wife? Did you see your kids? Did you call your parents? Text your sister? (And no, Facebook posts don't count.)

You have to live in the light. You have to engage with what matters. You have to live *with* those who are committed to living *with* you.

The friendships will come. The sand will fill the gaps. Just make sure the rocks are in there first.

Lesson 2: The "why" matters.

I've always been a "why" person. Since before I can remember, I have had an almost compulsive drive to understand things. For me, it has never been good enough to know that a thing exists or to know how to accomplish something. I need to know why. Why do you use this formula? Why do I need to vote? Why do I need to clean my plate?

My parents tell me that when I was very young, I wouldn't ask why. I would ask, "How come?" My mom loved to imitate how I would ask in that high-pitched little boy voice while pronouncing "come" like a whining child on a rollercoaster: "How cOOoome?" I don't remember doing this. I was very young, but suffice to say, I have always wanted to know why.

As I have grown older, I've learned that I am not in the majority of the population in this respect. Most people are ambivalent to the "why." They may or may not want to know the reason behind something, but, mostly, people are fine going about their lives accepting things as is or being upset with the way things are and never really thinking about what is causing those things in the first place.

That's ok. We don't have to understand everything. In fact, we are incapable of understanding everything. A big part of maturing is accepting and living in response to what is rather than getting wrapped up in what should be or what could be. It is ok to accept.

However... The "why" matters. In almost everything, the "why" matters a lot. The difference between lying and just being wrong is in why I say something. If I intended to deceive, I lied. If I told you what I thought was true, but it wasn't, I was just wrong. The reason I hire one person over another is either justified or discriminatory based on why I do it. Marrying someone out of love and commitment or because it increases my social standing completely changes the characteristic of the marriage. Having a drink as part of a meal or a social gathering and having a drink because I can't cope without it are significantly different behaviors.

Motivation, intention, reason. Whether we are aware of why we do things or not, the "why" is what shapes our lives. And this is hugely true in relationships.

Giving my wife flowers because I screwed up is a nice gesture, but at best, she will take it as a sign of remorse. At worst, she will see the flowers as a cheap way for me to brush off the way I hurt her. On the other hand, giving my wife flowers just because I love her, with no occasion or remorse attached, can be much more meaningful. The act is the same in both instances, but the "why" completely changes the characteristics of the act.

In relationships, the big rocks have to come first. I have to intentionally seek out interaction with the people in my life that I care about, but in this truth is an insidious trap. If I intentionally seek a relationship out of selfish motivation, it will eventually produce little fruit.

Start with God. What does God require of us? God wants us to do justice, love kindness, and walk humbly with him.[21] This is spelled out as clearly as can be in the Bible. The natural response for most of us is, "Ok. I can do that. I will be just. I will be kind…"

So, I go about my days doing the best I can. I treat people well. I try not to get angry, or at least not show it, while I'm driving. I give to charity. I vote. I recycle. I say please and thank you. I'm a good person. I'm definitely better than that jerk who just cut me off. I'm better than that politician I can't stand. I'm better than Kim Jong-Un. Dang! I'm not humble, though.

It isn't just that it's hard to do. It's impossible, and it comes down to the "why." Why am I trying to be just? Why am I trying to love kindness? If I am doing it out of duty or obligation, or, more likely, if I'm honest, if I'm doing it to earn favor with God, I'm not doing it at all. On the other hand, if I walk humbly with God, I will do justice and love kindness. If I start with the right heart attitude, the "why" becomes love. God loves justice. God loves mercy. If I love him, I want to do what he loves.

This is the tricky thing with God. The relationship only flows one way.[22] I'm not saying it isn't reciprocal. It is. But it is like a loop, like a circular pipe with a one-way valve. The water[23] only flows in one direction. If you mess up the order with God, it doesn't work. God is God, whether we like it or believe it or not. Our attitude toward him does not change who he is. But fortunately, he loves us and paid the price so that we can take our rightful place as his children.[24] And that is where our natural response comes in. A loving father inspires love and obedience. I love what he loves. I act as he would have me act.

The problem is that it does not work in the other direction. If I do as he would have me do, and I love what he loves, it does not make me his child. If I do these things to earn his love, it negates his sacrifice, which is the result of his love. If I try to earn right standing with God, I say he is not God but a counterpart in a transaction, and his love is now due to me. And now I have denied that he is God at all, for I am the one dictating the terms to him. Heavy stuff.

Unfortunately, this is also true of other relationships. You can't earn your wife's love. You can only love your wife and hope that she responds out of love. Anything else isn't love. Remember, love exalts. Love sacrifices. Love places the other first. When you act out of love, you cannot be thinking of your benefit from the action, or you are not acting out of love.

The question remains, though. So, what?! What do I do about it? All I can say here is try and identify something you can do for someone you love or someone you want to love better with no expectation of reward. Wash the dishes while no one is around, and do not call attention to it. Pray without asking for anything. Give without anyone knowing about it. Do what your spouse enjoys to do, and enjoy it, especially if you don't like to do it. Enjoy *their* enjoyment.

Sacrifice. Exalt. Submit. Walk humbly.

Lesson 3: Just do it.

Yes, the "why" matters, but getting too caught up on the reason behind everything can lead to paralysis. Sometimes you just have to jump in to get things rolling.

When I first started wrestling in junior high, I was pretty good. I was strong enough for my weight. I worked hard during practice, so I was pretty good at the moves we worked on. I hated losing and refused to quit. I did really well in practice. Then came my first match.

The ref blew the whistle to start the match, and I began processing all the information available to me. I wanted to do it right. I wanted to win. I was looking for the opportunity to shoot in and take my opponent down. I thought I knew counters to every known move (ignorance is bliss), so I was watching for my opponent to try something so I could drop him like a wet sack of laundry.

Then the ref blew the whistle again. "Warning green. Stalling."

Wait a second! I'm green. What do you mean, stalling?

We started again. Whistle. "Stalling green. One point awarded to red." *What?! We haven't even done anything yet.*

The referee leaned over to me and said, "You can't back away, son. You have to wrestle." I was so focused on countering or looking for the right opening, I was taking a couple of steps backward as soon as the ref blew his whistle. I didn't even realize I was doing it, but it wasn't that hard to fix. The next time, I focused on not going backward. I stood my ground, like a lighthouse in a storm. I was a rock, and a target that doesn't move is hard to miss.

I lost the match, but I learned a valuable lesson. Sometimes you just have to shoot in and see what it gets you. Sometimes, even when you don't see the outcome clearly, don't know if your motivation is right, or may be completely putting yourself at risk, you have to act. You have to just do it.

Many times, I pray, and the only real motivation is to try and get something from God. What's the alternative? Don't pray at all? And there are times when I just give my wife flowers because I screwed up. It doesn't really matter if my motivation is completely pure. It's the right thing to do. Pure of heart or not, I am working toward reconciliation.

Along the way, while I'm doing things for the wrong reasons, sometimes my heart changes mid-stream. I apologize to my wife because I was a jerk. But not really. I actually apologize to my wife because I want her to forgive me. I'm really just doing it because I don't want to be in trouble. I don't want her mad at me. It's all about me. But then she does. She forgives me, and I'm not thinking about me anymore at all. I'm thinking about her. I'm thinking about what an amazing woman I married and that I don't deserve her. My whole focus in that moment becomes Kari. Bingo: love.

It doesn't work this way every time. Sometimes I do good things for selfish reasons, and my attitude just stays selfish. However, sitting on my principles and waiting for my motivation to be pure and attitude to be correct before I act the way I know I should isn't better. It's worse.

Just spend time with your kids even if it is to get them to do what you want. Take your spouse out on a date even if you are just hoping for it to pay off later that evening. Have some quiet time in the morning with God, even if it feels like an obligation. Just do it.

Lesson 4: It's all about touches.

I'm not really a soccer fan. Just the wording of that statement probably hinted at it. If I was a soccer fan, I wouldn't call myself a soccer fan. I'd say, "football fan," and then smugly pause till you caught on. Or, I might say "soccer," but then correct the reading audience that the sport is really football. The whole world calls it football except us in the US. But I'm not really a fan, so I call it soccer and reply, "Heck yeah! 'Merica!"

Anyway, I'm not really a soccer fan, but I do think it's a good sport. Regardless of my own feelings about its entertainment value, I made all my kids play soccer.

The rule in our house was that you had to play soccer, whether you liked it or not, until you found something else that required you to move your body consistently for over an hour a day.

There really isn't a better sport out there for young people to get cardiovascular exercise than soccer. There are other great sports that offer opportunities for young people to get in great shape, but the best thing about soccer is that it takes almost no skill. A bad soccer player still runs around for an hour. The ball rolls! So even young, inexperienced players can just kick and chase.

All my kids played soccer until around third or fourth grade when each one found something else they wanted to do instead (grateful dad-moments, all). Four kids. Each of them started when they were four years old. My youngest played until he was nine. And I coached each one of them. Every year.

That's right. I'm not much of a soccer fan, but from 2004, when my firstborn played her first year of soccer, through 2016, my son's last year, I spent every fall on the soccer field (I won't call it a pitch), thirteen seasons of coaching a sport of which I'm not especially fond. But that wasn't really the point. I may not be fond of soccer, but I can see the value in it. And I can see why people love it. Regardless of how fond I am about the sport, I am really, really fond of my kids. So, I was a soccer coach.

That's where I learned about "touches." In other sports, in good old, red, white, and blue American sports, we call them "reps." Repetitions. Practicing. We say, "Again!" In soccer, they say "touches" (soccer always has to have its own word for everything).

The key to improvement is getting as many touches as possible. From the moment kids start playing, you want them to have a ball and dribble it around; dribbling, kicking, passing, shooting, scoring. They should touch the ball as often and as much as possible. Like the 10,000-hour rule to mastery from Malcolm Gladwell's book, kids need to have as much time with the ball as possible to become proficient at the sport.

Now really, this is just a catchy principle because as anyone with a brain knows, touching the ball doesn't necessarily lead toward exceptional control and manipulation in soccer. It isn't just about touches but quality touches. A player who toe-punches the ball over and over again is just ingraining a bad habit, not improving. So, the key is guiding and teaching the player in the fundamentals and principles of controlling the soccer ball and then... touches—quality touches.

The more rabid soccer fans out there may not believe it, but this wisdom isn't exclusive to soccer. Football, basketball, baseball, cello, ballet, financial modeling, writing, parenting, everything requires quality touches for improvement.

I took golf lessons about twenty-five years ago. They were really helpful. At the time, I was in my twenties, teaching and coaching football, didn't have any kids yet, and golfing pretty regularly. During that season of my life when I had more free time than I have had at any moment since, I would get out when the weather was decent and golf almost every week. I was scoring consistently around ninety, but I really wanted to get down into the low eighties. So, I took lessons.

The first thing the instructor asked me about were my goals. I explained the situation, what I was aiming to do, and how much I golfed, so he asked me, "If one of your football players said he wanted to improve and then said he would practice once every week or two for five months, so maybe ten to twelve times a year, what would you tell him?"

Ouch. Message received. I was not going to get significantly better at golfing without spending significant time with quality and intentional repetitions. And to do that, I was going to need to prioritize golf above other things in my life. I was going to have to do without some of the other ways I spent my time, and the reality was that I was simply not willing to place golf ahead of much of anything in my life. It wasn't a high enough priority to me. I changed my goal.

You simply will not get better at something without repetition. And repetition does not happen without commitment. And commitment requires sacrifice.

If I want to master a skill or concept, I have to consistently practice and work toward that goal. That will mean there will be times that I have to do it when I do not feel like it. It will mean that I will have to say "no" to other opportunities that conflict with my practice time. I have to commit. I have to sacrifice.

The word for this is discipline. Whether it is a cross-over dribble or my marriage, discipline is required for improvement, and it does not come naturally.

Sure, some relationships start organically. You meet someone at the grocery store, and you hit it off. You feel attraction. You enjoy their company. It is totally organic and no work is involved. It is all upside, but here is the nasty little secret about our universe: It is falling apart. The natural state of things is not creation and life. The natural state of things is entropy, atrophy, and decay. Left on its own, everything dies, including relationships. The eventual outcome of organic relationships is that they will end.

Schedule it. Calendarize it. Commit to it. My relationship with my kids will move further apart without intentional effort to keep them close. My marriage will wither. My friends will move on in life. My walk with God will become a lonely stroll by myself. Without intentional sacrifice, consistent effort, and regular interaction, relationships die. They all require discipline because we all need touches. (See what I did there?)

Big rocks. Focus on your "why." Do it anyway. Discipline. Written that way, it sounds simple, and I guess it is. These are four simple concepts. However, simple and easy are not the same thing. How do you win an Olympic gold medal in the hundred-meter? Run faster than everyone else. Simple. Hard.

I'd like to say I'm a relationship expert. I'd like to say that after figuring all this out, the implementation of it was the easy part. That just isn't true. Living in the light with people, discerning how far someone can be realistically trusted, and learning how to walk with God on a daily basis, these things are really hard, and I fail at them more often than I succeed.

The concepts and practices may be simple, but they are incredibly difficult to implement in life. Just the first one—putting the most important things first gets all mixed up as soon as you try to put it into practice. My wife and children are some of my biggest relational rocks. Part of the love that I have for them requires sacrificing my time to work and provide for them. Part of that love requires that I emphasize and prioritize my children's education. The result is that I spend significantly more of my life around the people that I work with than the people that I love. How do you balance that? How do you keep the sacrifice from taking priority over the reason for the sacrifice?

Oh yeah! Keep the "why" in mind. Ok. Remember why I'm working. Remember who I'm doing this for. But, I think maybe I'm actually doing it for me. I want the money. I like the challenge. I need the security. When did that happen? When did the sacrifice become an indulgence?

It doesn't matter. Just do it. Just work and remember the original "why" even if it isn't always true anymore. Now, go home and take your wife on a date. Intentionally interact with her. Do it weekly. Make it a regular thing. Discipline. You can do this.

But there's football practice this week. And it's been a long day. And I'm tired. I just want to watch a show and go to bed. The guys are playing poker tonight. Shoot! Big rocks. I'm not fitting in the big rocks... Rinse and repeat.

This is the part that has always driven me crazy. I'll learn something important. I'll learn something that should alter my life. And I genuinely believe it to be true, so I would like to live my life in accordance with this knowledge. Nine times out of ten, though, I just don't. I want to do what I know to be right, but I do something else.[25] And even when I get it right, it doesn't seem to last. At some point along the way, I just forget.[26] That's ok, though. That is the point. The only way[27] to navigate this life is to rinse and repeat. Keep going back to lesson one: the big rock.[28]

If this was a self-help book, I'd be explaining what to do next. I'd be breaking down a system for you to implement this in your life, but I can't do more than point you in the right direction because if you haven't realized it yet, this isn't a self-help book. This is a you-need-help book.

Notes

Not all references to the Bible are explicit in this book. That is to say that throughout this book, I sometimes reference an idea that is in the Bible, but it wouldn't be accurate to say it was a Bible reference. Other times it is. There are a few direct references that I include here, but in this section, I try and refer you to some corresponding verses that are parallel or in agreement to what I have discussed in the book. I would encourage you to look them up in context.

All verses here are listed in the ESV (English Standard Version) translation.

Endnotes

1. Do you not know that in a race all the runners run, but only one receives the prize? So run that you may obtain it. Every athlete exercises self-control in all things. They do it to receive a perishable wreath, but we an imperishable. So I do not run aimlessly; I do not box as one beating the air. But I discipline my body and keep it under control, I pummel my body and make it a slave lest after preaching to others I myself should be disqualified. (1 Corinthians 9:24-27)

2. I press on toward the goal for the prize of the upward call of God in Christ Jesus. (Philippians 3:14)

3. Count it all joy, my brothers when you meet trials of various kinds, for you know that the testing of your faith produces steadfastness. And let steadfastness have its full effect, that you may be perfect and complete, lacking in nothing. (James 1:2-4)

4. Come now, you who say, "Today or tomorrow we will go into such and such a town and spend a year there and trade and make a profit"— yet you do not

know what tomorrow will bring. What is your life? For you are a mist that appears for a little time and then vanishes. (James 4:13-14)

5   What father among you, if his son asks for a fish, will instead of a fish give him a serpent; or if he asks for an egg, will give him a scorpion? If you then, who are evil, know how to give good gifts to your children, how much more will the heavenly Father give the Holy Spirit to those who ask him! (Luke 11:11-13)

6   But even the hairs of your head are all numbered. (Matthew 10:30)

7   And he said, "Go out and stand on the mount before the Lord ." And behold, the Lord passed by, and a great and strong wind tore the mountains and broke in pieces the rocks before the Lord, but the Lord was not in the wind. And after the wind an earthquake, but the Lord was not in the earthquake. And after the earthquake a fire, but the Lord was not in the fire. And after the fire the sound of a low whisper. (1 Kings 19:11-12)

8   …And behold, I am with you always, to the end of the age. (Matthew 28:20)

9   Then the Lord God said, "It is not good that the man should be alone; I will make him a helper fit for him." (Genesis 2:18)

10   I have said these things to you, that in me you may have peace. In the world you will have tribulation. But take heart; I have overcome the world. (John 16:33)

¹¹ These are the generations of the heavens and the earth when they were created, in the day that the Lord God made the earth and the heavens. When no bush of the field was yet in the land and no small plant of the field had yet sprung up—for the Lord God had not caused it to rain on the land, and there was no man to work the ground, and a mist was going up from the land and was watering the whole face of the ground— then the Lord God formed the man of dust from the ground and breathed into his nostrils the breath of life, and the man became a living creature. And the Lord God planted a garden in Eden, in the east, and there he put the man whom he had formed. And out of the ground the Lord God made to spring up every tree that is pleasant to the sight and good for food. The tree of life was in the midst of the garden, and the tree of the knowledge of good and evil. A river flowed out of Eden to water the garden, and there it divided and became four rivers. The name of the first is the Pishon. It is the one that flowed around the whole land of Havilah, where there is gold. And the gold of that land is good; bdellium and onyx stone are there. The name of the second river is the Gihon. It is the one that flowed around the whole land of Cush. And the name of the third river is the Tigris, which flows east of Assyria. And the fourth river is the Euphrates. The Lord God took the man and put him in the garden of Eden to work it and keep it. And the Lord God commanded the man, saying, "You may surely eat of every tree of the garden, but of the tree of the knowledge of good and evil you shall not eat, for in the day that you eat of it you

shall surely die." Then the Lord God said, "It is not good that the man should be alone; I will make him a helper fit for him." Now out of the ground the Lord God had formed every beast of the field and every bird of the heavens and brought them to the man to see what he would call them. And whatever the man called every living creature, that was its name. The man gave names to all livestock and to the birds of the heavens and to every beast of the field. But for Adam there was not found a helper fit for him. So the Lord God caused a deep sleep to fall upon the man, and while he slept took one of his ribs and closed up its place with flesh. And the rib that the Lord God had taken from the man he made into a woman and brought her to the man. (Genesis 2:4-22)

12 Two are better than one, because they have a good reward for their toil. For if they fall, one will lift up his fellow. But woe to him who is alone when he falls and has not another to lift him up! Again, if two lie together, they keep warm, but how can one keep warm alone? And though a man might prevail against one who is alone, two will withstand him—a threefold cord is not quickly broken. (Ecclesiastes 4:9-12)

13 Now faith is the assurance of things hoped for, the conviction of things not seen. (Hebrews 11:1)

14 And this is the judgment: the light has come into the world, and people loved the darkness rather than the light because their works were evil. For everyone who does wicked things hates the light

and does not come to the light, lest his works should be exposed. But whoever does what is true comes to the light, so that it may be clearly seen that his works have been carried out in God. (John 3:19-21)

[15] But if we walk in the light, as he is in the light, we have fellowship with one another... (1 John 1:7)

[16] They have all turned aside; together they have become corrupt; there is none who does good, not even one. (Psalm 14:3)

[17] All we like sheep have gone astray; we have turned— every one—to his own way... (Isaiah 53:6)

[18] So he went and hired himself out to one of the citizens of that country, who sent him into his fields to feed pigs. And he was longing to be fed with the pods that the pigs ate, and no one gave him anything. "But when he came to himself, he said, 'How many of my father's hired servants have more than enough bread, but I perish here with hunger! (Luke 15:15-17)

[19] "Behold, the virgin shall conceive and bear a son, and they shall call his name Immanuel" (which means, God with us). (Matthew 1:23)

[20] Everyone then who hears these words of mine and does them will be like a wise man who built his house on the rock. And the rain fell, and the floods came, and the winds blew and beat on that house, but it did not fall, because it had been founded on the rock. And everyone who hears these words of mine and does not do them will be like a foolish

man who built his house on the sand. And the rain fell, and the floods came, and the winds blew and beat against that house, and it fell, and great was the fall of it. (Matthew 7:24-27)

21 He has told you, O man, what is good; and what does the Lord require of you but to do justice, and to love kindness, and to walk humbly with your God? (Micah 6:8)

22 Abide in me, and I in you. As the branch cannot bear fruit by itself, unless it abides in the vine, neither can you, unless you abide in me. I am the vine; you are the branches. Whoever abides in me and I in him, he it is that bears much fruit, for apart from me you can do nothing. (John 15:4-5)

23 Jesus answered her, "If you knew the gift of God, and who it is that is saying to you, 'Give me a drink,' you would have asked him, and he would have given you living water." (John 4:10)

24 for you were bought with a price... (1 Corinthians 6:20)

See what kind of love the Father has given to us, that we should be called children of God; and so we are... (1 John 3:1)

25 For I do not understand my own actions. For I do not do what I want, but I do the very thing I hate. (Romans 7:15)

26 For if anyone is a hearer of the word and not a doer, he is like a man who looks intently at his natural

face in a mirror. For he looks at himself and goes away and at once forgets what he was like. (James 1:23-24)

27 Jesus said to him, "I am the way, and the truth, and the life. No one comes to the Father except through me. (John 14:6)

28 Simon Peter replied, "You are the Christ, the Son of the living God." And Jesus answered him, "Blessed are you, Simon Bar-Jonah! For flesh and blood has not revealed this to you, but my Father who is in heaven. And I tell you, you are Peter, and on this rock I will build my church, and the gates of hell shall not prevail against it. (Matthew 16:16-18)

CPSIA information can be obtained
at www.ICGtesting.com
Printed in the USA
LVHW101447210422
716756LV00002B/4